crosstraining for endurance athletes

BUILDING STABILITY, BALANCE, AND STRENGTH

crosstraining for endurance athletes

BUILDING STABILITY, BALANCE, AND STRENGTH

RAUL GUISADO

BOULDER, COLORADO

Crosstraining for Endurance Athletes

Disclaimer
Before embarking on any strenuous exercise program, including the training described in this book, everyone, particularly anyone with a known heart or blood-pressure problem, should be examined by a physician.

Printed in the United States of America.

10 9 8 7 6 5 4 3 2 1

Distributed in the United States and Canada by Publishers Group West.

Library of Congress Cataloging-in-Publication Data

Guisado, Raul.
Crosstraining for endurance athletes / Raul Guisado.
p. cm.
Includes index.
ISBN 0-9746254-0-X (pbk. : alk. paper)
1. Endurance sports—Training. 2. Sports injuries—Prevention. 1. Title.
GV749.5.G85 2004
613.7'11—dc 22

2004022972

An imprint of VeloPress®
1830 North 55th Street
Boulder, Colorado 80301–2700 USA
303/440-0601 • Fax 303/444-6788 • E-mail velopress@insideinc.com

To purchase additional copies of this book or other VeloPress® books, call 800/234-8356 or visit us on the Web at velopress.com.

Cover design: Rick Griffith, MATTER, with Anita Koury
Interior design and composition by Anita Koury
Cover photos by Chris Milliman, www.chrismilliman.com
Interior photos by Don Karle

contents

To my wife Kendra and to our parents:
Evelyn, John, Donna, Raul, Becky, and Ray.

introduction

Everyone has limits on the time they can devote to exercise, and cross-training simply gives you the best return on your investment—balanced fitness with minimum injury risk and maximum fun.

—Paula Newby Fraser

Why should endurance athletes crosstrain? Most of us struggle as it is to find enough time during the week to train our sport. We have been led to believe that the best way to improve our performance in our particular sport is simply to train that sport more, and he or she who trains the most wins, right? Wrong. You also need to train smarter in order to maximize your time and energy. And, as I'll show you in this book, crosstraining isn't just for athletes in sports like soccer, football, skiing, tennis, and basketball. Endurance athletes such as runners, cyclists, mountain bikers, swimmers, triathletes, and Nordic skiers can benefit greatly from devoting a moderate percentage of their training time to crosstraining.

If applied correctly, functional and integrated training can help endurance athletes reach their potential and achieve their goals. The application of the proven crosstraining methods employed in other sports is long overdue for endurance sports participants. Many athletes in endurance sports develop imbalances as a result of repeating the same movements for several hours every week. In time, these imbalances lead to decreased performance and eventually injury. These imbalances can be prevented and/or corrected through an effective crosstraining program.

We can also enhance performance and prevent injury by training beyond the demands of our sport. In other words, we can prepare our muscles, joints, and connective tissue to deal with forces greater than those they are subjected to when we run, swim, skate, and ride. We all have strengths, and, unfortunately, we all have weaknesses or limiting factors. In many instances, the most effective way to overcome these limiting factors is to stimulate our nervous system to make physiological adaptations through crosstraining.

Ultimately, the objective of this book is to help you think critically about how you spend your training time and convince you of the importance of developing a crosstraining program based on your individual goals, needs, wants, and abilities. I aim to empower you with knowledge that will allow you to create a customized crosstraining plan all your own. The more tailored your training program is to your specific needs, the faster, stronger, more agile, and more powerful you'll become!

chapter 1
integrated crosstraining

Adventure isn't hanging on a rope off the side of a mountain. Adventure is an attitude that we must apply to the day-to-day obstacles of life—facing new challenges, seizing new opportunities, testing our resources against the unknown, and in the process, discovering our own unique potential. —*John Amatt (organizer and participant in Canada's first successful expedition to the summit of Mount Everest)*

FUNCTIONAL, INTEGRATED, AND SPORT-SPECIFIC TRAINING

Before we discuss how we can enhance our performance and prevent injury through crosstraining, let's make sure we're speaking the same language. The approach to crosstraining for endurance sports described in this book can be best described as functional, integrated, and sport-specific.

Functional training refers to a focus on improving function. In other words, a functional training program is concerned with trying to prepare an individual for specific physical demands. Such a program is in stark contrast to the type that most bodybuilders follow, which is more aesthetics driven. An example of functional training would be when a physical therapist prescribes exercises for someone who is hurt on the job and is trying to return to work. The therapist would recommend movements that would help prepare muscles, joints, ligaments, and tendons for the forces and ranges of motion required by that individual's occupation.

An *integrated training* approach is one that trains the nervous system to recruit various joint and trunk stabilizer muscles during movement. As the name implies, the goal is to train muscles in coordination with other muscles so that movement will be more efficient. For example, a single-leg squat could be described as an integrated exercise because it involves the recruitment of various stabilizers of the ankle, knee, hip, and trunk while at the same time strengthening the primary mover muscles of the knee and hip.

Sport-specific training simply refers to a training approach that will in some way benefit an individual's ability in a particular sport. Sport-specific training can involve the attempt to simulate the movements of the sport such as a basketball player performing a vertical jump. However, sport-specific training can also refer to any strength, power, agility, coordination, stability, flexibility, and energy system training designed to enhance performance in a specific sport. For instance, if a football player wanted to make an interval workout as sport-specific as possible, he would exert himself at the same intensity and for the same duration as he does during a game. He would rest the same amount of time between efforts as occurs during the average huddle and total break in the action.

Integrated, functional, and sport-specific training involves multiplanar, multijoint, and multidimensional movements. This approach to crosstraining is dynamic, progressive, and systematic and continually challenges the nervous system. Training programs of this nature are varied on a regular basis in order to force the body to adapt to differing planes of motion, ranges of motion, type of resistance, body positions, intensities, tempos, durations, sets, repetitions, frequencies, and rest periods.

Functional, integrated, and sport-specific training are all interrelated and complement one another. All three approaches involve training movements as opposed to simply training muscles. In other words, muscles are trained in "integration" rather than isolation. Training muscles in isolation has been the traditional approach to crosstraining in many sports for several years. It's difficult to truly train any muscle in complete isolation, but many of the fixed and stable machines you see in any gym have been designed to emphasize or target one or two major muscles. For instance, a leg extension machine attempts to "isolate" the quadriceps muscles of the upper leg. This machine is a great example of the more traditional approach to crosstraining as it's designed to be very stable and requires that the exerciser be seated as she extends her legs against resistance. This results in little necessity for other muscles in the body to be recruited.

Let's say you're a soccer player and want to strengthen the quadriceps muscles to improve the force with which you kick the ball. The leg extension machine can definitely be useful in overloading the muscle by emphasizing this primary mover. However, your strength could be enhanced if during the strengthening exercise you could also train the stabilizers of the exercising leg as well as those of the trunk, ankle, knee, and hip of the opposite leg.

Consider that instead of sitting in a leg extension machine you stood on one leg and put an ankle strap on the opposite leg, which was attached to a cable that lifted a weight stack. As you extend the exercising leg, you contract not only the quadriceps muscles but also the stabilizing muscles of the ankle, knee, and hip of that leg. In addition, you force stabilizers of the trunk and opposite leg to be recruited in order to provide the exercising leg with a solid platform from which to produce force.

The less stable exercise is more functional in that you can move the exercising leg in a full range of motion that will prepare the joints, muscles, and connective tissue for the act of kicking. It also requires the nervous system to coordinate or integrate the recruitment of various stabilizer muscles used when you kick a soccer ball. Lastly, the less stable exercise is more sport-specific in that it more closely approximates and better prepares the body to kick a soccer ball with more force.

I will concede that the more stable leg extension machine can be a great tool to strengthen the quadriceps muscles, and because of its greater stability, it allows the exerciser to work under a higher resistance load. However, it is as important to train the stabilizers that will provide the platform for that kick to fire in the right amounts in concert with the primary movers.

If you can create a more stable platform, you can produce more force because a higher percentage of the muscle fiber of the primary movers can be dedicated to, in this case, kicking and a lower percentage to stabilizing. The less stable exercise also helps you prevent injury by training all of the stabilizers in the kicking motion to deal with rotational, gravitational, and lateral forces under a load.

I'm not proposing that the leg extension machine be totally cut out of the soccer player's training program. I am merely saying that this athlete could also benefit greatly from incorporating some exercises that are more functional, integrated, and sport-specific. Perhaps some days the soccer player would begin her resistance training workouts by training movements, and as various stabilizers became fatigued, she could strengthen primary movers in relative isolation. For other workouts, the athlete could fatigue primary movers first and then challenge her nervous system to still stabilize her trunk and joints effectively.

So, what does all of this have to do with endurance sports? Functional, integrated, and sport-specific crosstraining can be even more effective and beneficial for athletes who perform the same movement for long periods of time. It's vital that you prepare your body beyond the forces, stressors, and demands of your sport by performing movements other than those you repeat over and over again. This approach will result in your trunk and joints becoming more stable, which in turn will increase efficiency and force production with every stride, pedal stroke, skate, or swimming stroke. Ultimately, this type of crosstraining will enhance performance and decrease your risk for injury.

ENDURANCE SPORT INJURIES

Endurance athletes experience numerous types of injuries. What follows are descriptions of some of the most common.

Plantar Fasciitis

The *plantar fascia* is a band of tough and fibrous tissue that runs from the heel to the toes on the bottom of the foot. *Plantar fasciitis* is a result of the plantar fascia becoming inflamed. Pain is felt in the arch of the foot, usually closer to the heel. This is a common overuse injury among endurance athletes and is related to poor biomechanics of the foot, weak muscles on the bottom of the foot, tight calf muscles, and ankle inflexibility.

Ankle Sprains

Numerous ligaments surround the ankle joint. An ankle sprain results when these ligaments become overstretched or torn. The most common cause of ankle sprains is rolling the foot inward when running on an uneven surface. When the sole of the foot is forced inward, body weight causes stress to the ligaments stabilizing the outside of the ankle joint. Ankle sprains are most common among athletes with poor ankle and knee biomechanics, ankle inflexibility, and ankle instability.

Shin Splints

The *tibialis anterior* is a muscle located on the front of the shin. Shin splints occur when the muscle fascia along the edge of the tibia becomes inflamed as a result of repeated stress. When this fascia becomes inflamed, pain is felt along the lower half of the shin every time the tibialis anterior muscle contracts due to increased pressure in this area. Shin splints are considered an overuse injury related to tight and weak calf muscles and poor ankle and knee biomechanics.

Knee Injuries

Knee injuries are common among all endurance athletes. The numerous tendons and ligaments that surround the knee joint can become stressed, and other soft tissue in and around the joint can become inflamed. Patellar pain syndrome is one example of an overuse injury marked by pain underneath the kneecap. Most knee injuries can be linked to poor ankle, knee, and hip biomechanics as well as knee instability.

Hamstring Injuries

The *biceps femoris,* or hamstring muscles, are located on the back of the upper leg. These muscles can become strained under high tension loads during strenuous exercise such as sprinting or while accelerating uphill. The hamstrings can also become injured as a result of small repeated tears over an extended period of time, as in an especially long event. Hamstring injuries are often linked to poor warmup; lack of flexibility of the hamstring, buttocks, and lower-back muscles; and poor posture and biomechanics of the pelvis, knee, and spine.

Iliotibial Band Friction Syndrome

The *iliotibial* band runs along the outside of the thigh from the pelvis to the tibia just below the knee. Primarily a stabilizer during any endurance sport, it can become irritated from overuse. Pain is usually felt on the outside of the knee or lower thigh. Iliotibial band syndrome is caused by poor posture and biomechanics of the foot, knee, and pelvis; inflexible thigh and buttocks muscles; and weak external hip rotator muscles.

Hip Injuries

The hip is a large joint supported by numerous muscles, tendons, and ligaments. Two common hip injuries among endurance athletes are greater trochanteric bursitis and iliopsoas tendinitis. *Greater trochanteric bursitis* is caused by repetitive sliding of fascia in the hip joint over the greater trochanter or head of the femur. Pain is felt inside the hip joint and in the muscles responsible for hip abduction. *Iliopsoas tendinitis* is an overuse injury that causes pain in the muscles responsible for hip flexion. Endurance athletes with poor lower-body mechanics and posture, weak trunk musculature, and muscle strength and flexibility imbalances are at risk for experiencing hip injuries.

Lumbar Spine Injuries

The lumbar spine, or lower back, has to deal with significant forces during any endurance sport. Endurance athletes can experience overuse injuries in the form of muscle strains to the lower back muscles, vertebral disc tears and ruptures, and stress fractures of the vertebrae. All of these injuries can be related to poor posture and biomechanics; instability of the ankle, knee, hip, and shoulder; weak trunk musculature; spine and pelvis instability; and tight hamstrings, buttocks, and lower back musculature.

Shoulder Injuries

The shoulder joint is surrounded by various muscles, tendons, and ligaments that allow for a large range of motion. Shoulder injuries are most common among swimmers, who may experience rotator cuff soreness, inflammation, and tendinitis. The most common cause of shoulder injuries is poor swimming stroke mechanics. If a swimmer has an inadequate amount of shoulder roll during his stroke, the rotator cuff muscles get squeezed by the bones in the joint. Shoulder injuries can also be a result of poor posture, lack of stability, and poor flexibility and strength in the muscles that surround the shoulder joint.

Neck Injuries

The neck is surrounded by large and small muscles in the shoulders and back as well as numerous tendons and ligaments. All of this soft tissue works together to stabilize the vertebrae in the neck in order to support the weight of the head during flexion, extension, and rotation. Neck injuries can be experienced by all endurance athletes, and pain can be felt in various locations. Muscle spasms are common in the trapezius muscles, and tendinitis can develop in many areas of the neck. Neck injuries are often the result of poor posture, muscle weakness, and strength imbalances.

PREVENTING INJURY

If you've been an endurance athlete for a few years, you've probably already experienced some sort of repetitive use–type injury to the muscles, tendons, or ligaments surrounding your ankles, knees, hips, or shoulders. At first you ignored the acute twinges of pain or muscle spasms and chalked them up to common fatigue. Before long, you endured more prolonged periods of pain, inflammation, and eventually decreased range of motion of the affected joint. Finally, the injury evolved from a minor discomfort to a chronic state of soreness, tightness, and nagging pain that prevented you from training on a regular basis.

If you have yet to deal with such an injury or want to avoid being sidelined in the future, you're in luck, because the knowledge and crosstraining strategies discussed in this book can help you prevent repetitive use injuries and keep you active.

First, it's important to understand how these injuries develop. All of the tendons, ligaments, muscles, bones, and nerves in the body are interrelated and are affected by imbalances elsewhere in the body. We can develop all sorts of strength and flexibility imbalances between the left and right sides and front and back of our body. Postural stress, tissue overload, repetitive movement, lack of core stability, and lack of neuromuscular efficiency can all lead to muscle imbalances.

Endurance athletes are very prone to developing such imbalances because they perform the same movement over and over again. For example, it's common that certain muscles will become stronger than others because they get more use when you perform a particular sport. Stronger muscles tend to shorten or become tighter than weaker muscles. If we don't take measures to stretch these tighter muscles or strengthen the weaker ones, we quickly create imbalances in the body that affect posture and fluid, efficient movement. When our posture is altered and the range of motion of joints is compromised, we develop compensatory habits that eventually lead to injuries.

When we're imbalanced or out of alignment, dysfunctional movements occur and tissue becomes overloaded or stressed. This results in less neuromuscular control, decreased performance, and eventually injury. Any dysfunctional or compensatory movements lead to the integrity of soft tissue such as muscles, tendons, and ligaments being compromised because of abnormal distorting forces. If one part of the body is out of alignment, then other parts of the body have to compensate in attempts to balance the weight distribution of that dysfunctional area during movement.

For instance, a golfer rotates repetitively from either right to left or left to right depending on her dominant side. In the short term, a young golfer can get away with neglecting the other side of her body. However, to prevent postural and other imbalances that lead to injury, the golfer will need to strengthen and stretch all of the stabilizers and primary movers on her nondominant side.

Now, take a look at your particular sport. What if the muscles of your chest were stronger and tighter than your back muscles, or the muscles that surround one side of your hip were considerably tighter than the other side, or your biceps femoris (hamstrings) were significantly weaker than your quadriceps (thigh muscles)? Chances are your posture and optimal running stride, skate, pedal stroke, or swimming stroke for your anatomy would be affected. If these imbalances had existed for countless workouts, you would unknowingly have adapted your technique to compensate for these discrepancies in either strength or flexibility. You would now become so comfortable and accustomed to this altered stroke, stride, or skate that you'd be unaware that certain muscles, tendons, and ligaments were being overloaded with forces greater than they have been engineered to handle. In essence, the stability of certain joints had become compromised. As you would progress in the sport, you'd increase the volume and intensity of your workouts, and ultimately these imbalances would present themselves in the form of soft-tissue injuries such as tendinitis or muscle strains.

So, what's the key to preventing these imbalances in the first place? It all starts with proper posture. When you exercise with poor postural alignment, you may develop muscle imbalances and joint dysfunctions that can lead to injury. Optimum posture and alignment help prevent distortions and provide optimal shock absorption, weight acceptance, and transfer of force during functional movements. Proper posture and alignment provide structural and functional efficiency to the myofascial (soft tissue), articular (bones), and neural (nerves) systems of the body. The central nervous system coordinates neuromuscular control as it receives information from these three systems. In other words, the appropriate motor program is chosen to perform an activity. This ensures that the right muscle contracts at the correct joint, with the proper amount of force, at just the right time. If certain muscles are tighter or weaker than others, or if a joint is dysfunctional, neuromuscular control suffers.

This condition in turn decreases stabilization, force production, and force reduction. When our ability to stabilize is inhibited, we decrease efficiency and disperse and diminish forces poorly. Moreover, stabilization directly affects our ability to produce force. When force production is diminished, performance decreases significantly. Lastly, if our soft tissue is unable to reduce the forces we incur during movement or to decelerate our mass adequately, we greatly multiply our risk for injury. In endurance sports, a lack of stability and an inability to reduce force will ultimately lead to a breakdown at the weakest or most vulnerable link in the movement chain.

Ultimately, poor posture and muscle imbalances result in the inhibition of muscles responsible for movement, leading to compensation and substitution by stabilizers. This compensation and imbalances between muscles that are strong and shortened and others that are weak and lengthened can result in altered joint alignment. Muscle tightness creates a lot of joint problems, whereas muscle weakness allows them to worsen. Muscle tightness, muscle weakness, joint dysfunction, and decreased neuromuscular efficiency can all eventually lead to injury.

The best way to prevent these imbalances from sidelining us is to incorporate functional, integrated, and sport-specific flexibility as well as trunk and joint stability and strength movements into our crosstraining programs.

ENHANCING PERFORMANCE

Okay, enough about preventing injury. How do we become faster? Well, integrated, functional, and sport-specific crosstraining might just be what will get us over a performance plateau and take us to the next level.

All endurance sport athletes can benefit from improving efficiency. It's a simple equation: Added propulsion for the same amount of effort equals an increase in speed. So, how do we improve efficiency? One way is to improve technique. And, we know that improving our posture and the length–tension relationships between various muscles can facilitate technical developments. Fluid movement starts with posture and an optimum balance between strength and flexibility.

We can also benefit from an increased ability to produce force. Force production, however, is dependent on stability. If we're unable to provide our extremities with a solid platform, how can we expect to produce maximal force? In other words, the more stable your trunk and joints are, the better you can utilize the strength and power you possess. Why? Because any movement we perform involves the recruitment of what we call *primary* movers and stabilizers. This means certain muscles are best put to use as primary movers or force producers, and others are best utilized to stabilize our center of mass and joints. When we increase the ability of stabilizing muscles to do what they do best, a higher percentage of the muscle fibers in our primary movers can be dedicated to force production. Thus, even if you don't make any gains in strength, improved stability will result in an increase in your ability to produce force.

Functional, integrated, and sport-specific crosstraining can be very effective in improving both efficiency and force production. This approach to crosstraining not only will result in strength and power development but also teaches the nervous system how to better stabilize your trunk and joints at the same time so that you can improve efficiency and force production. It is this emphasis on improving stability and training the nervous system to recruit muscles in just the right amounts for a given movement that will ultimately allow you to train beyond the demands of your sport and reach your potential.

chapter 2 flexibility

Better to bend than break. *—French proverb*

IMPORTANCE

Optimal movement requires flexibility. To maintain certain body positions, it's imperative that you're not only strong and stable but also flexible. Take yoga, for example—it requires more energy for a novice to get into and hold even the most basic of poses than someone who has been practicing yoga for years. The same holds true in any physical endeavor. An inflexible athlete is more prone to injury and expends more energy during movement than a flexible one. The more active you are, the more important it is that you stay flexible.

POSTURE

Efficient movement begins with good posture and the ability to maintain a *neutral spine,* or your spine's natural curvature. When you're in such a position, the discs between the vertebrae in your spine are pressured the most evenly from left to right and front to back. This position also provides your arms and legs with the best possible platform from which to move and produce maximal force.

This neutral position means that your ears are lined up with your shoulders and that your pelvis is level in relation to your spine. To find this position, stand with your back against a wall. Ideal posture would require that your head, shoulders, and butt are all touching the wall. The thickest part of your hand should get stuck between the wall and your lower back. If your hand can slide all the way through this space, then your pelvis is tilted too far forward, resulting in excessive lumbar curvature. If the thickest part of your hand can't slide far enough, then your pelvis is rotated too far back.

Flexibility affects posture and the ability to find and maintain a neutral spine. If certain muscles are tight in relation to others, this condition can result in our head being too far forward, our shoulders rounded, or our lower back being curved excessively or too little.

When muscles are tight and posture is poor, movement is compromised. Movement is the most fluid and efficient when large primary mover muscles can be used mainly for movement and very little for stabilization. When our muscles are tight and posture is affected, tendons, ligaments, and stabilizer muscles lose their ability to stabilize our trunk and joints properly. This state ultimately results in an increased risk for injury and decreased performance.

INJURY PREVENTION

Some of the most common injuries among endurance athletes are sprains and strains of the foot, ankle, knee, hip, lower back, shoulders, and neck. All of these types of musculoskeletal injuries can be minimized or prevented by increasing flexibility. Being strong with stable joints does you very little good in terms of injury prevention if you're inflexible. Stretching can help reduce stress on joints and allow them to handle greater forces without suffering significant trauma. In all sports, flexible athletes are less likely to get injured, and strong athletes who don't stretch are usually the first to get injured. This is because as a person gains muscle mass, he or she generally needs to stretch more frequently to maintain flexibility.

PERFORMANCE

Besides injury prevention, maintaining your overall flexibility is an important element of performance. We need to stay limber in order to be able to maintain proper postural and joint alignments when we're trying to produce force. Every movement we perform has what are called *biomechanically advantageous positions*. In other words, when bones are aligned properly, you'll have the best platform from which to utilize maximal muscle strength. When we're inflexible, joints can become misaligned, resulting in a loss of energy. Tight muscles can also affect optimal ranges and paths of joint motion. And, when these ranges are limited or paths are altered, primary movers become less efficient. For example, tight hamstrings can affect the length of a runner's stride and a cyclist's pedal stroke and result in less force production by their quadriceps.

LENGTH-TENSION RELATIONSHIPS

Muscles, tendons, and ligaments all have what are referred to as *optimal length–tension relationships*. In other words, if our soft tissue is shortened or lengthened under or beyond a certain point, the tension of the tissue is altered. Once this ideal length–tension relationship between various muscles, tendons, and ligaments is lost, posture, movement, and performance can all suffer. For instance, when our pecs are stronger and tighter than our rhomboids and lats, we end up with a rounded shoulder posture. If we become accustomed to this postural position, movements that involve trunk stability or the shoulder joint will be more labored. Finally, our performance in any endurance sport will be negatively affected because they all require trunk stabilization and some form of shoulder movement and stability.

SYMMETRY

To maintain optimal length–tension relationships, we need to strengthen and stretch all our muscles. This will help us maintain fore and aft and lateral symmetry. If we neglect the muscles on the front or back and left or right of the body, we'll develop imbalances that can affect our performance. In other words, we must stretch all of the major muscles in our body each time we stretch. We thus need to develop enough body awareness to be able to identify differences in flexibility between the left and right sides and front and back of our body.

Basic Kinesiology

The major muscles that are most important for endurance athletes to stretch are labeled in the illustrations.

UPPER-BODY MUSCLES

Biceps brachii (bis)—located on the front of the upper arm

Deltoids (delts)—shoulder muscles

Latissimus dorsi (lats)—attach at the back of the upper arm and fan down the back

Pectoralis major (pecs)—run along the chest

Rhomboids—located between the shoulder blades

Trapezius (traps)—attach on the back of the skull and fan down the shoulders

Triceps brachii (tris)—located on the back of the upper arm

MAIN TRUNK STABILIZERS

Erector spinae (back extensors)—run along length of the spine

Internal and external obliques—run at angles across the midsection

Rectus abdominis (abs)—run vertically along the front middle of the torso

Transverse abdominis (TVA)—muscular ring around the lumbar spine

LOWER-BODY MUSCLES

Adductor longus (adductors)—run along the inner thigh

Gastronomes and soleus (calves)—run behind the lower leg

Gluteus maximus (glutes)—the large and powerful buttock muscles

Biceps femoris (hamstrings)—run behind the upper leg

Hip flexors—various muscles around the hip joint

Quadriceps (quads)—various muscles on the front of the upper leg

Tibialis anterior (tibs)—run along the front of the shin

WHEN AND HOW TO STRETCH

Even relatively sedentary people should make a habit of stretching at least five to ten minutes per day. Active individuals and athletes should spend five to ten minutes stretching lightly before exercise and ten to fifteen minutes of deeper stretches after exercise. All stretching will be safer and more effective if it follows

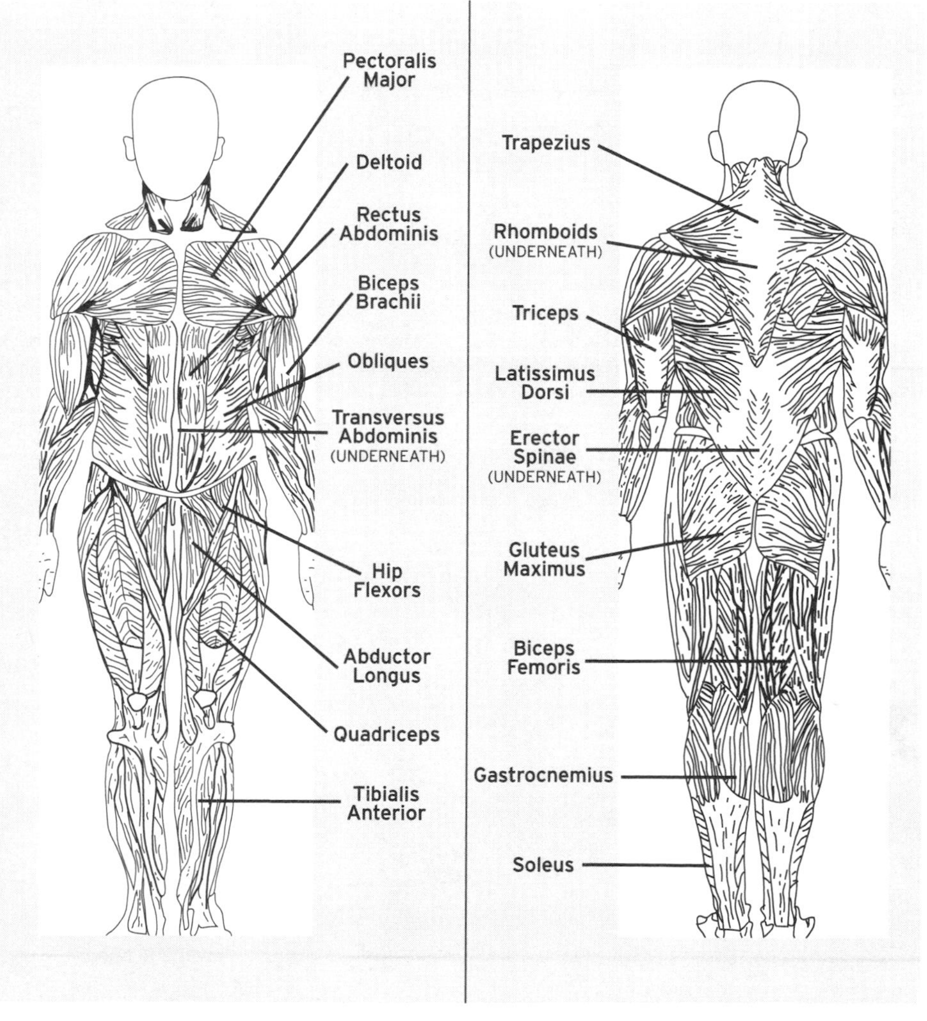

at least five minutes of light to moderate aerobic exercise. Light exercise increases blood flow to the musculature and results in greater elasticity. People who are genetically less flexible will need to spend more time and energy stretching to become flexible. In addition, as we get older, most of us will need to commit more time to stretching to maintain our flexibility.

There are two main ways to stretch: passively and actively. *Passive* stretches, the most common type, are when the stretch is deepened slowly, gradually, and in a controlled manner. A passive stretch should be held for between ten and thirty seconds depending on how tight the muscle is and the desired goal of stretching. It's also helpful to take full, slow, and deep breaths while stretching passively. This will make the experience more relaxing for you and allow you to deepen the stretch slightly with each exhale. Passive stretches can be done before and after exercise.

Much more advanced, *active* stretches are when muscles and supporting soft tissue are taken to full ranges of motion during specific movements. Stretching actively requires above-average flexibility, joint stability, and body awareness. Examples of active stretches would be a walking-forward or lateral lunge or throwing a two- to three-pound medicine ball against a trampoline. The advantage of this type of stretching is that you can increase the amount of blood flow to soft tissue while you stretch. This makes active stretching most beneficial when performed before a workout as it can enhance your preparation for exercise. On the other hand, it's more difficult to control a stretch when it's done actively, which in turn will increase the risk of injury while stretching. As a result, I have the athletes I work with only stretch actively under my supervision and only once I'm thoroughly convinced that their body is prepared to meet the demands of the movement.

Stretching should not be painful or too strenuous or involve jerky or bouncing movements. The last thing we want to do is injure a muscle that we'll need when we train! It's also important to be careful not to overstretch a muscle that's not tight. Our goal is to increase or maintain flexibility in order to improve range of motion, regain symmetry, and enhance performance. Stretching beyond a muscle's capability can eventually lead to compromised stability and function.

Stretches

What follows are some passive stretches that can be easily done almost anywhere. How deep a stretch is taken and the amount of time it is held will depend on your degree of flexibility and athletic needs.

2.1 | **Delts:** While standing, hold onto something and lean forward, keeping your arm bent.

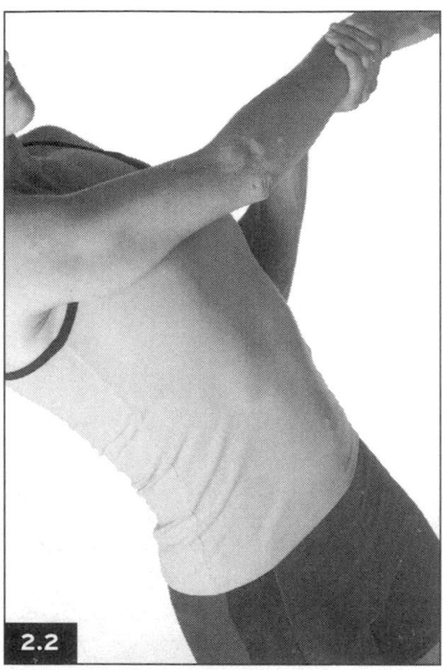

2.2 | Lats: Pull your arm straight in front of your body, and pull your elbow with the opposite arm.

2.3 | Rhomboids: While standing and holding onto a fixed object, pull away from the object and turn your torso.

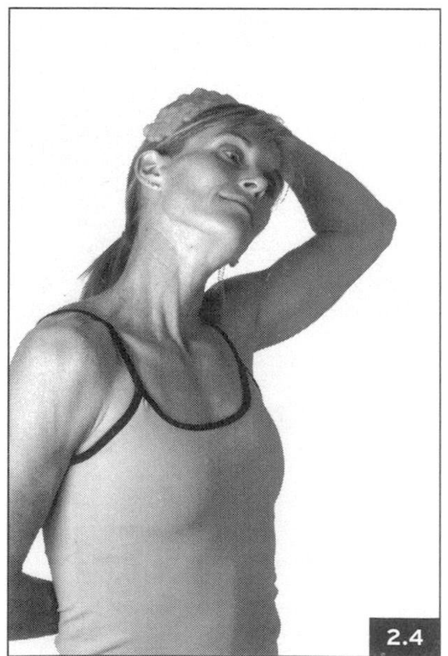

2.4 | Traps: Pull your head forward and to the side with one hand while your opposite hand is behind your back.

2.5 | Pecs and Bis: While standing, hold onto something and lean forward while keeping your arm straight.

2.6 | Back Extensors: While kneeling, flex your spine forward and push your weight back onto your feet.

2.7 | Obliques: While standing with a wide stance, flex your spine laterally, first in one direction, then the other. You can work your tris while still standing by bringing your arm above your head and pulling on your elbow with the opposite arm.

2.8 | Abs: While lying facedown, arch your upper body up by pushing with your arms.

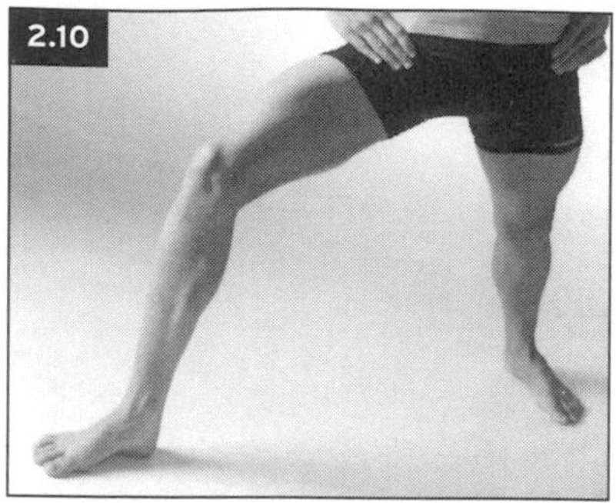

2.9 | Groin: While sitting, bring your feet together with your knees bent, and push your knees toward the floor.

2.10 | Adductors: From a lateral lunge position, put more weight on one leg, with the opposite leg straight.

2.11 | Glutes: Lie on your back, bring your knees up, and pull the knee of your crossed leg toward the opposite shoulder.

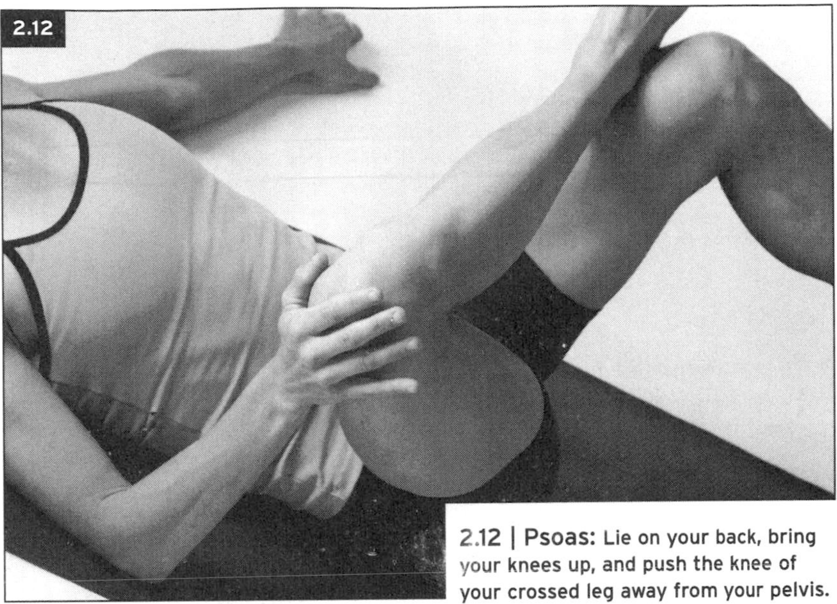

2.12 | Psoas: Lie on your back, bring your knees up, and push the knee of your crossed leg away from your pelvis.

2.13 | Iliotibial Band (IT Band): While lying on your back, raise one straight leg in the air; keep your hips on the floor, and pull your foot with a belt or rope inward toward the floor.

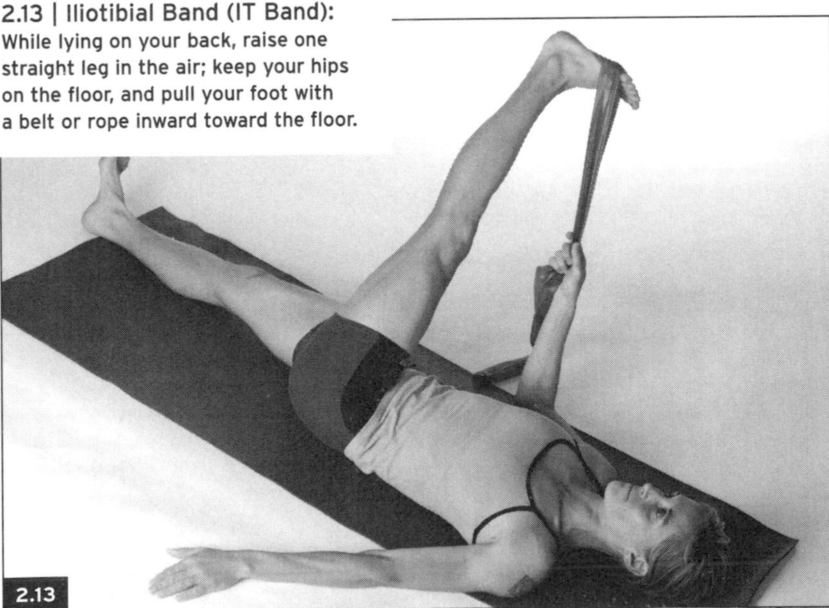

2.14 | Hamstrings: Put your heel at hip level, keep your leg straight, and bend forward at the waist. To work your quads, return to a standing position and pull your heel to our glute.

2.15 | Hip Flexors: From a kneeling position, push your hip forward and keep your chest back.

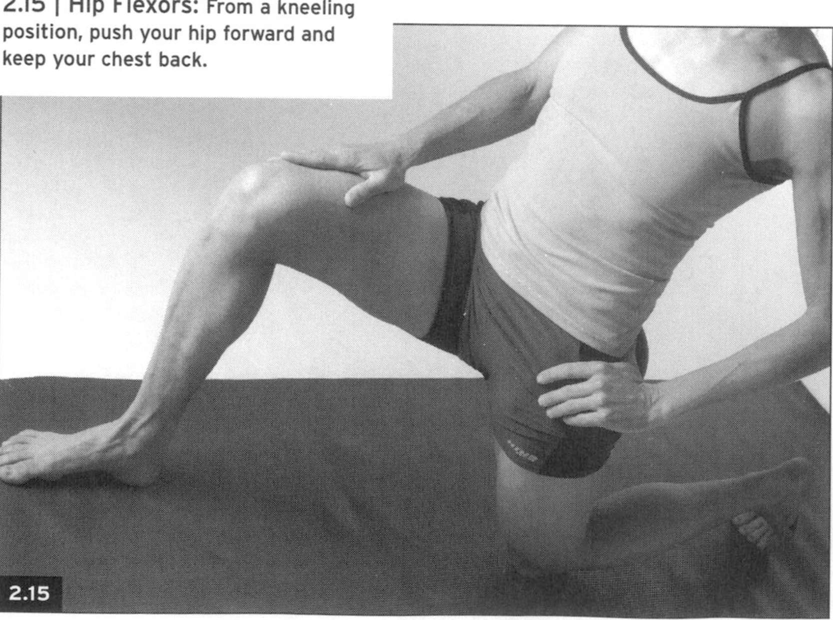

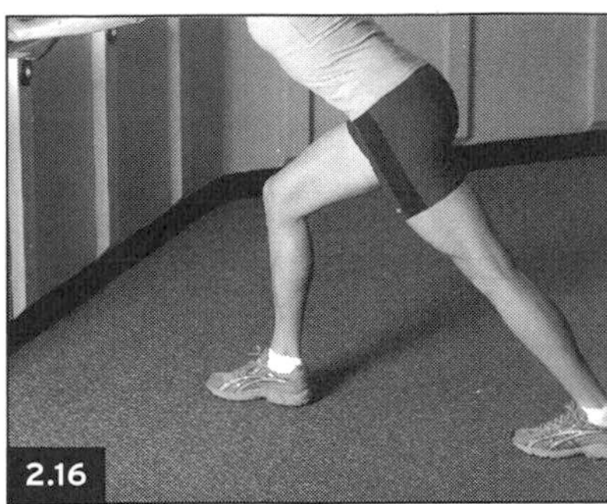

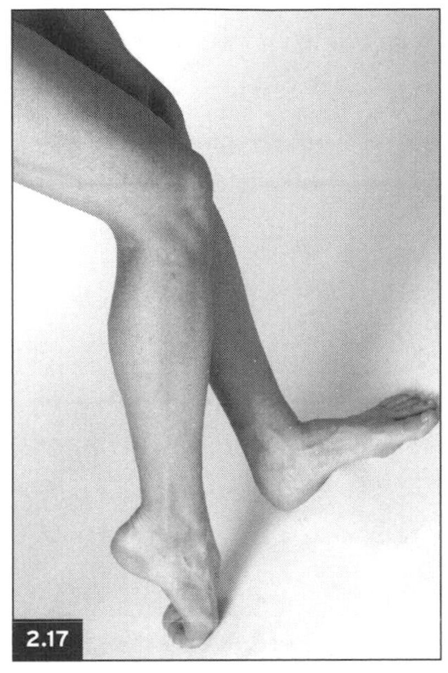

2.16 | Calves: Lean your upper body forward, keep your feet flat on the ground, and stretch with your knee straight and flexed.

2.17 | Tibs: While standing, roll your toes underneath your foot and lean forward.

2.18 | Multiple-Muscle Stretch (lats, back extensors, obliques, and glutes): While lying on your back, turn your hips to one side and extend your leg to the floor while keeping your shoulders on the floor.

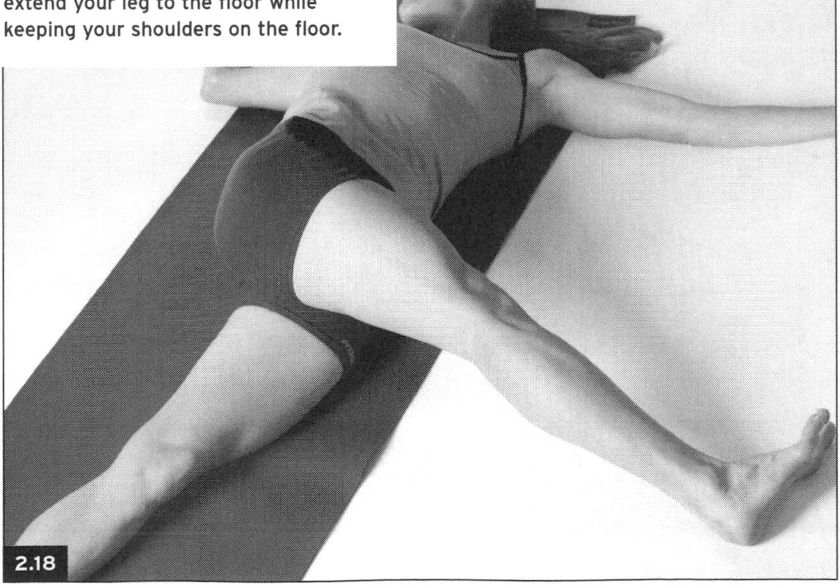

YOGA

Yoga classes and videos can be a very effective way to increase your flexibility. However, be cautious with poses that go beyond your muscles' stretching capabilities. Such positions can actually stress joint capsules and supporting tendons and ligaments, which in turn may lead to joint instability and inflammation.

To use yoga safely and effectively, you'll want to do some research and seek out instructional videos, books, or classes that match your goals, needs, wants, and abilities. As with any pursuit, think critically about what you're trying to accomplish. If you're practicing yoga with the goal of improving or maintaining your flexibility, then you won't need to go to extremes.

MASSAGE

Many types of massage can help keep muscles flexible by lengthening and increasing blood flow to tissue. Getting massages on a regular basis can also release toxins and lactic acid from the muscles and aid in recovery. A lot of high-level athletes in a multitude of sports use massage as a way to help keep both their muscles and their mind relaxed. I recommend finding a licensed massage therapist who works with athletes and is within your price range. Massage services at spas, for example, tend to be costly and not geared toward the needs of athletes.

Pre-event massages, within forty-eight hours of competition, should be relatively light and invigorating. Deeper massages can be very beneficial as well but can cause temporary muscle soreness; as a result, they should be scheduled two to three days before an exceptionally strenuous workout or event.

AS YOU AGE

As I mentioned earlier, flexibility generally decreases as we get older. Therefore, we need to dedicate more time to stretching as we age merely to maintain our muscle elasticity.

Lessened flexibility is due to a variety of factors but is accelerated when people are sedentary and neglect their bodies. As a result, staying flexible will not only help you move better and prevent injury but will also keep you feeling young.

chapter 3
trunk stability

You can't shoot a cannon from a canoe. —*Paul Chek (on the importance of core strength in athletics)*

The trunk or core of your body is the point from which your extremities (arms and legs) are connected. When you engage in physical activity of any kind, the platform for your strength, power, and control comes from your core. Everything you do—from reaching into the trunk of your car to pick up a heavy bag of groceries, to leaning over the sink when you brush your teeth—involves the core musculature to some degree.

Trunk stability refers to the ability to coordinate the recruitment of the musculature that attaches to your spine and pelvis to maintain optimal postural positions during movement. Dynamic balance sports such as skiing, snowboarding, and surfing require a high degree of trunk stability to control the body's center of mass and to make it easier for lower-body stabilizers to react to terrain and gravitational forces. And, efficiency, injury prevention, and force production in endurance sports such as running, cycling, and swimming are all dependent on the ability to stabilize the spine and pelvis for hours at a time.

Trunk Strength and Stability Roles

Transverse abdominis—helps stabilize center of mass at the lumbar spine

Internal and external obliques—aid in lateral flexion and rotation of the spine and act as stabilizers of the spine in these two planes

Rectus abdominis—are responsible for spinal flexion and provide fore and aft spinal stability

Erector spinae—are responsible for spinal extension and provide fore and aft spinal stability

Lattisimus dorsi—provide pulling strength for the arms and act as shoulder and torso stabilizers

Rhomboids—are responsible for shoulder retraction, shoulder stability, and thoracic spine stability

Pectoralis—provide pushing strength for the arms and act as shoulder and torso stabilizers

Gluteals—provide lower-body strength and act as stabilizers of the pelvis

Hip flexor complex—are responsible for hip flexion and hip joint stability

Hip abductors and adductors—are responsible for hip abduction and adduction and hip joint stability

Biceps femoris—provide pulling strength for the legs and act as pelvis stabilizers

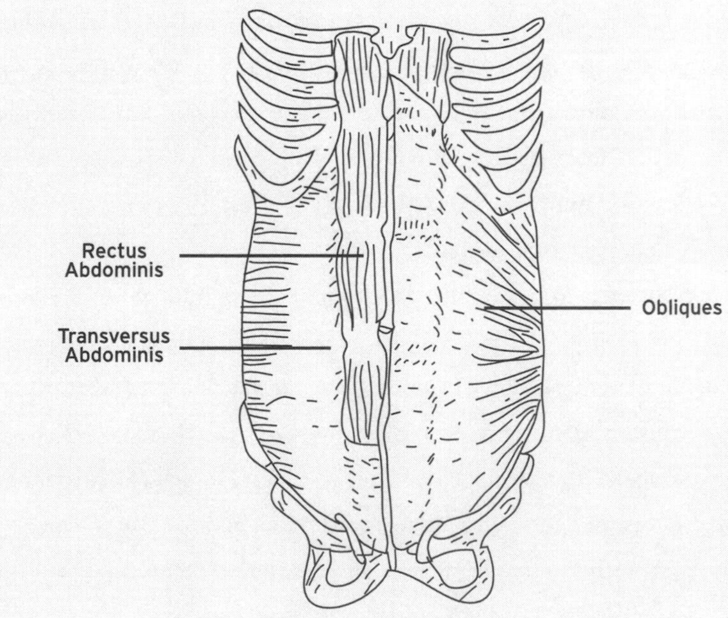

Developing a stable trunk requires strong core musculature. However, many athletes in various sports have trunk strength but are not stable. This is because stability is dependent on the ability of the nervous system to recruit these muscles during movement. Moreover, most athletes are training their core musculature in isolation opposed to integration. Endurance athletes need to incorporate trunk stability training into their weekly programs to eventually teach these muscles to contract and effectively stabilize the pelvis and spine during their sport.

ANATOMY OF THE TRUNK

The most important trunk muscles are the transverse abdominis (innermost abdominal wall), the internal and external obliques (side abdominals), the rectus abdominis (large outer muscles of the abdomen), erector spinae (smaller back musculature), the lattisimus dorsi (large back musculature), the rhomboids (smaller back muscles between the shoulder blades), the pectoralis (chest), the gluteals (buttocks), the psoas, rectus femoris, and tensor fascia latae (commonly known as the hip flexor complex), the hip abductors and adductors (outer and inner thighs), and the biceps femoris (hamstrings). Optimal strength, power, and balance require that these muscles work together to stabilize the core when we move.

POSTURE AND NEUTRAL SPINE

The term *neutral spine* refers to the position in which all the vertebrae are level in relation to one another. The spine runs from your head to your pelvis and has a natural curvature.

The spine has three major portions. The *cervical* spine is essentially your neck, the *thoracic* portion is where your ribs attach, and the *lumbar* section is the lower back. The spine curves toward the rear of the body in the upper back and curves forward at the lumbar region. When it's in this neutral position, it is best able to disperse loads, provides a strong foundation for movement, and places

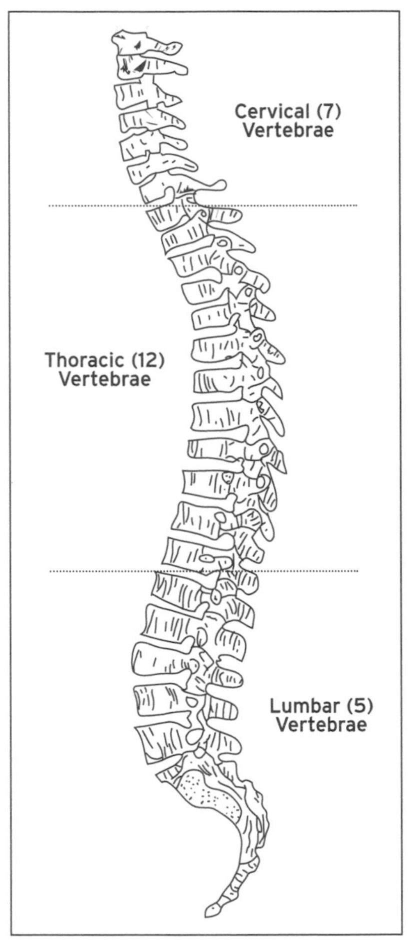

the least amount of pressure on vertebral discs. The vertebral discs are made of soft tissue and act as mini-shock absorbers in our back. If we're not in a neutral spine position, the vertebrae may be squeezing a disc, making it more prone to injury during movement. As a result, it's important that we learn how to find and maintain this neutral spine position when we sit, walk, run, lift, swim, ride, and perform any movement that may involve loading or rotation of the spine.

Many of us have developed poor postural habits and positions over the years that our tendons, ligaments, and muscles have become accustomed to. Breaking such habits may take a great deal of stretching muscles that are tight, usually the chest musculature, and strengthening muscles that are weaker, generally the muscles of the back. Little did your parents know that reminding you not to slouch would not only make you look more respectable but would help keep your back healthy as well as improve your performance!

TRAINING TRUNK STABILITY

We can improve our trunk stability by increasing our awareness of how these muscles function in various movements and making an effort to involve those muscles when we crosstrain. We will discuss specific exercises that accomplish this goal very effectively. Another way to improve trunk stability is to integrate these muscles when we are strengthening other muscles in our lower and upper body. When you integrate core musculature into your resistance training program, you're teaching the body, and more specifically the nervous system, to recruit these muscles when performing a variety of movements. As a result, you'll be able to prevent injury, move more efficiently, and create a more stable base from which you can exert your strength and power during all kinds of physical activities.

This approach is also known as *functional training* because you're preparing the body for realistic movements that you make in your sport and in everyday activities. For example, the leg press machine that can be found in nearly every large gym in the world is great for building quadriceps (thigh muscle) strength. However, unless you're a circus performer (you know, the guy who lies on his back and juggles large barrels with his feet), it's not very functional. A more functional lower-body exercise, for most activities, would be to perform a standing single-leg squat while holding a medicine ball, dumbbells, or a weighted plate.

Functional resistance training can also greatly reduce an athlete's risk of injury. For example, it's common to see ankle and knee injuries in sports like basketball and tennis that involve quick direction changes. Oftentimes these injuries could have been avoided by preparing the body for the demands of the sport by improving overall strength and stability in all planes of movement. Endurance athletes experience repetitive or overuse type injuries because they tend to overlook the need for training their bodies in side-to-side or rotational movements. Failure to incorporate such movements into your training program can cause muscle and postural imbalances. Ultimately, we want to improve our strength in all planes of movement in order to increase power and efficiency through improved balance and stability.

What does this have to do with your trunk? Well, to perform a single-leg squat while holding dumbbells, with proper form, your core musculature has to be recruited to keep your pelvis level, maintain your posture, and stabilize your center of mass so that you don't fall over. In other words, the functional exercise will not only fatigue the quadriceps just as effectively as the leg press machine but also train all of the stabilizing muscles of the trunk, pelvis, hip, knee, and ankle at the same time. I am not proposing that you stop using the leg press machine or any other stable machine that was developed to emphasize and strengthen a particular muscle. I am merely stressing the need for incorporating the concept of integration into your resistance training.

By improving the ability to stabilize the spine and pelvis, you accomplish three main things. First, trunk stability protects the spine from trauma. Holding the spine in a biomechanically advantageous position and activating abdominal and back musculature during movement can prevent a variety of rotational and impact injuries to your spine and help keep your back healthy for life.

Second, as mentioned previously, trunk stability improves balance. Balance is enhanced by joint stability. The better you can stabilize every joint in your body, the better you'll be able to control movement. Human center of gravity or mass is slightly below and behind the navel. Thus, the better we can stabilize that point, the more effectively we can make subtle balance adjustments in our extremities. Most important, a stable core will make it easier for other joints to handle stresses and as a result help prevent injury.

Third, trunk stability increases strength and power. It's necessary to provide a solid platform from which the muscles of the extremities can maximally produce force. A strong and stable trunk allows a muscle to devote more energy to movement and less energy acting as a stabilizer. The more complex or powerful the movement, the more important trunk stability becomes.

DEVELOPING CORE STRENGTH

Stability of the trunk is dependent on core strength. Popular exercises such as crunches are just one of many ways to strengthen the abdominal and back musculature. However, such exercises only recruit very specific musculature.

It's imperative to go one step further by performing movements that simultaneously strengthen multiple core stabilizers in order to maximize trunk strength and stability.

We want to strengthen the muscle groups that stabilize our skeletal structure. For example, the muscles in the thoracic area determine your posture in each sport and help connect your upper and lower body. Trunk stabilizers don't have the ability to drive you forward, but they are the base from which your arms and legs work. We need this platform in order to maintain proper running and cycling posture. In developed swimming movements, especially, it can be even more important. Your torso can actually contribute force through rotation as the direction of force from arms and legs oppose each other. Consider how a fish moves when it swims. Its fins and tail don't move independently from the rest of its body. The force that a fish creates is through longitudinal flexion of its whole body. Similarly, a swimmer with a strong core will be more efficient and able to produce more force.

As we develop core strength and stability, we can increase body awareness of individual and small groups of muscles. This awareness is the first step in improving imbalances in posture and correcting form issues. For instance, as we discussed earlier, many of us have poor posture that can negatively impact our endurance sport performance. The first step to improving your posture is being able to contract individual back muscles effectively by performing specific exercises to strengthen them. As you develop greater body awareness and strength, you will be better able to perform movements that require recruitment of multiple trunk stabilizers as you work postural muscles. In other words, you'll train your body to use these muscles simultaneously in sport-specific movements while maximizing your time and energy by fatiguing primary movers and stabilizers at the same time.

Forward propulsion in any endurance sport is limited by your weakest muscular link. For example, even if you have the legs of a power lifter, you must have the strength in your upper body to control the force these muscles can produce. When you ride a bike, gravity dictates that all down force generated is limited to your body weight and the opposing action of pulling up on the opposite crank arm. However, you can increase down force by pulling up on the handlebar, thus opposing the tendency for your body to rise as you extend your legs. But, since your legs are attached at your hips, the stable platform your arms create must be extended to your hips and legs through your trunk. There are similar benefits of having a strong and stable trunk in the sports of running and swimming.

When you become fatigued running, swimming, or cycling, your form falls apart. It's not just because of tired legs but also tired arms and a tired back. Having a strong torso helps hold your form together in the latter stages of any endurance effort.

A variety of techniques have developed to strengthen the core and develop the movements that will enhance performance in endurance sports such as running, cycling, and swimming. The basic concept is to apply a factor of instability to exercises we already do, as well as adding specific exercises to develop trunk strength and stability.

For instance, instead of sitting on a bench and performing a dumbbell arm curl, perform the same exercise while standing on one leg. Now your trunk musculature is forced to stabilize your pelvis and spine and help keep the weight centered from side to side and front to back. This is the most basic approach. More advanced core training involves standing, kneeling, or sitting on unstable surfaces such as a stability ball, balance board, or foam roller.

If you've ever seen those big colored balls at the gym, those are stability balls, and hundreds of exercises involve their use. Consider a normal dumbbell bench press on a standard weight lifting bench. Now, replace the bench with a stability ball, with the ball resting between your shoulder blades. You perform the normal bench-pressing movement, but now your core muscles are acting to stabilize and balance your body to keep the weight in the correct center as you perform the exercise.

TRANSVERSE ABDOMINIS

For the majority of people, the transverse abdominis (TVA) is the most neglected and detrained of the trunk musculature. As the inner abdominal wall, it can also be described as the body's "natural weight belt." This muscle connects to the thoracolumbar fascia of the back to form a ring around the core at the navel. Unlike all of the other muscles described in this book, this muscle doesn't attach to any bones. As a result, it's not designed to bring two bones together as your biceps brings your lower arm closer to your upper arm. In other words, the TVA is purely a stabilizer and not responsible for movement.

Because your center of mass is below and behind your navel, this muscle plays a huge role in all aspects of stability. The human torso is capable of so much movement in this area, and endurance athletes need to take advantage of all the stability help they can get. The more we can control spinal forward flexion, extension, lateral flexion, and rotation during movement, the better we can control our mass. When we control our mass better, we allow primary movers to spend more energy producing force and less energy stabilizing. The end result is—you guessed it—an increase in efficiency and performance.

Merely learning how to activate the transverse abdominis can improve trunk stability and balance immediately. The goal is that, eventually, the body will become accustomed to contracting this "natural weight belt" prior to performing any movement. As a result, you will be better able to stabilize your lower back, protecting it from injury and also providing a stronger platform for your arms and legs.

Pulling the belly button in toward the spine can activate the transverse abdominis. This is not to be confused with sucking in your gut. Activation of the TVA should result in a narrowing around the entire waist and a downward slope from the sternum or breastbone to the navel. Through training and awareness, everyone can learn to coordinate the contraction of the TVA with every movement. At first, drawing the navel in before performing an exercise might feel awkward and difficult, but soon it will become both comfortable and habitual. It's possible to continue to breathe normally and deeply in spite of drawing the navel inward. However, deep breaths while activating the TVA require more expansion of the midthoracic region of the chest. This exercise takes a little practice in order to keep from elevating your shoulders when you take a full breath, but it will feel increasingly more natural.

LEARNING HOW TO ACTIVATE THE TVA

One of the easiest ways to learn how to activate the TVA is through the recruitment of the lower abdominal muscles. While lying faceup, with knees bent and feet flat on the floor, place a pair of folded socks or something similar under the small of your back. Try to relax your entire body, especially your

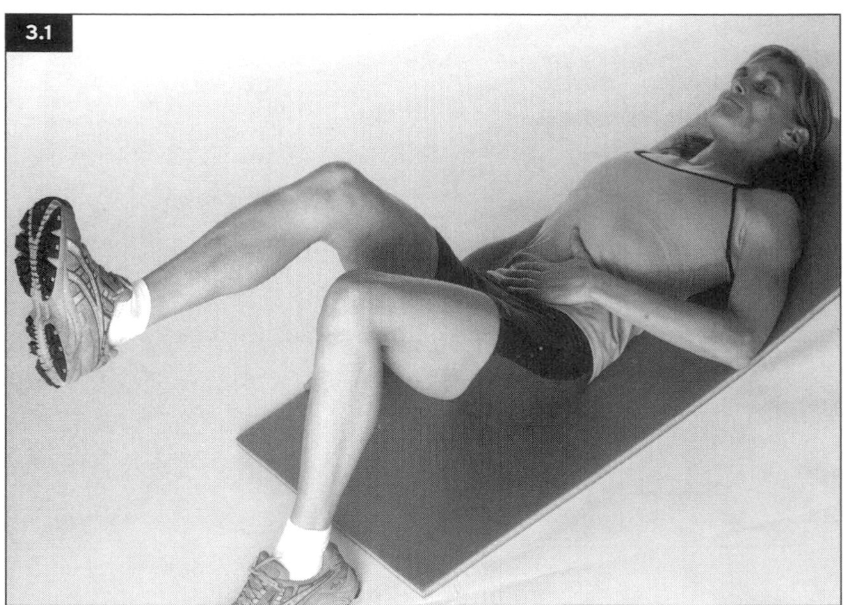
3.1

legs and shoulders. Now draw in your navel, keeping one hand around your waist and the other on your belly. You should feel your midsection narrow and a downward slope from your chest to your hips. Alternate lifting each bent leg off the ground, without losing pressure on the pair of socks. Be sure not to move your pelvis or affect the downward slope and narrowed waist.

If your lower abdominals or TVA are very weak, you'll find it difficult to keep your pelvis from moving when you lift your foot.

If this exercise seems or becomes very easy, try it with a straight leg or with both legs bent simultaneously. Stellar lower abdominal strength and transverse activation would be to lower both straight legs at the same time from ninety degrees to the floor and up again without allowing your lower back to arch.

TRUNK STABILIZATION AND STRENGTH EXERCISES

All trunk strength and stability movements should be done cautiously, with a neutral spine position and by first activating the transverse abdominis. It's important to develop a high level of TVA awareness and strength in order to protect the lower back even during the easiest exercises. All but the movements designed to develop power should be performed in a slow and controlled manner. It's recommended that all exercises be done on a soft surface, in an open area, and that a spotter be used for safety when attempting to stand on an elevated and very unstable surface such as a foam roller or stability ball.

TRUNK STABILITY EXERCISES

3.2

3.2 | Dynamic Bridging on Stability Ball: With one foot on the floor and your shoulders and head on the ball, slowly raise and lower your hips.

3.3 | Dynamic Quadruped: Kneel on all fours; alternate extending your opposite arm and leg straight out.

3.4 | Kneeling on Stability Ball: Kneel on the stability ball, maintaining a neutral spine with no break at your waist.

3.3

3.4

3.5 | Single-Leg Kick While Bridging on Ball: With your feet on the floor, your shoulders and head on the ball, alternate extending one leg straight out and to the side.

3.6 | Single-Leg Stability Ball Pikes: In a push-up position with one foot on the ball, extend your hips straight up in the air.

TRUNK STRENGTH EXERCISES

3.7 | Double-Leg Lowering: Lying faceup on the bench with your hips at one end, slowly lower your bent legs toward the floor and back up.

3.8 | Crunches over Stability Ball: With your feet on the floor and your lower back supported by the ball, extend your back over the ball slowly and crunch up.

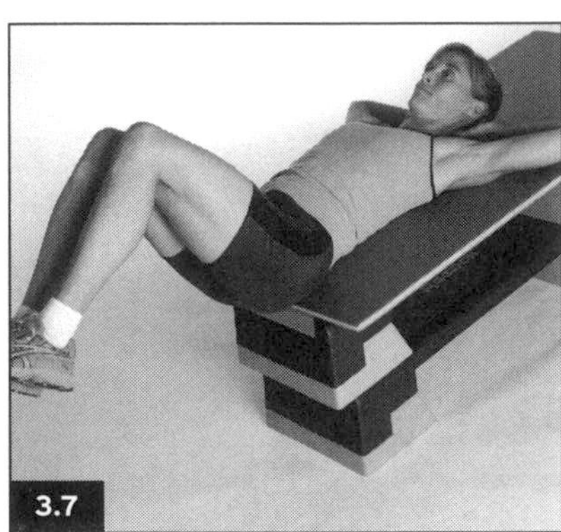
3.7

3.8

3.9 | Side Crunches over Stability Ball: With your feet on the floor and one hip on the ball, laterally extend over the ball slowly and crunch up.

3.9

3.10 | Forward Leg Roll-outs on Ball: From the push-up position, with your feet on the ball, flex and extend your legs.

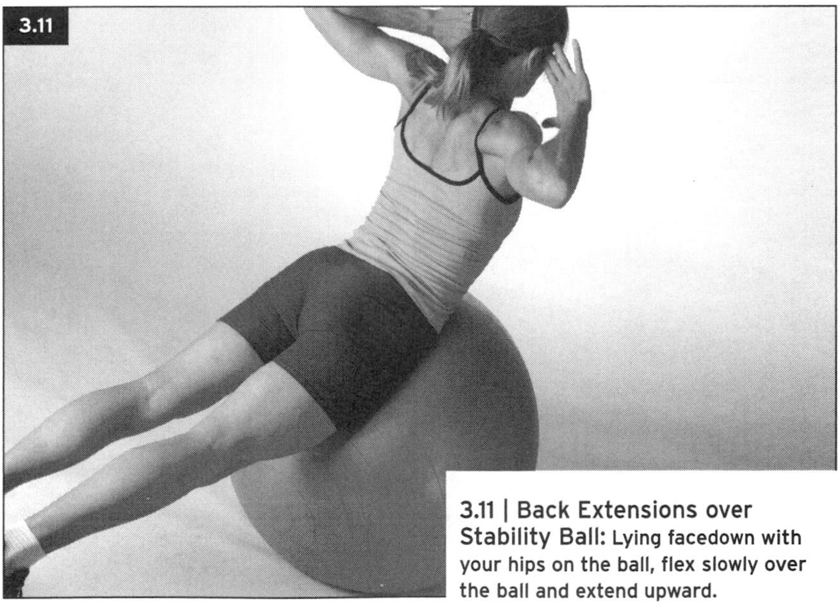

3.11 | Back Extensions over Stability Ball: Lying facedown with your hips on the ball, flex slowly over the ball and extend upward.

TRUNK POWER EXERCISES

3.12 | Stability Ball Sprinter Pops: From the push-up position, with your feet on the ball, alternate explosively flexing and extending a single leg on and off the ball.

3.13a,b | Explosive Oblique Cable Pulls: Stand sideways to the cable, and explosively pull the cable from low to high; maintain a neutral spine and relaxed traps.

3.13a

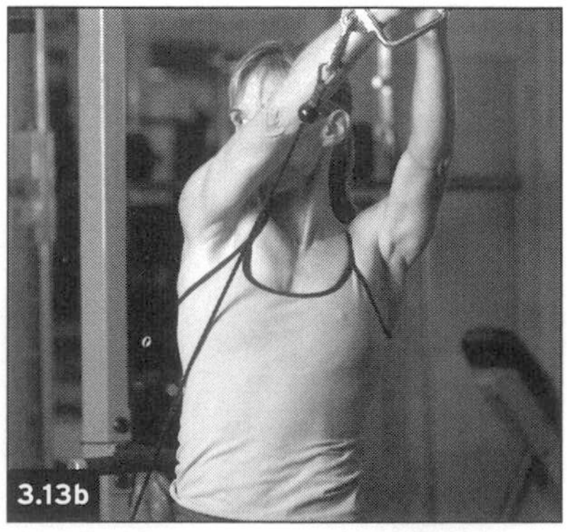

3.13b

OTHER TRUNK POWER EXERCISES

Explosive Medicine Ball Back Extensions: Lying facedown on a bench with your hips supported, break at your waist slowly with a neutral spine and, holding a medicine ball, extend up, explosively throwing the medicine ball to a partner at various angles.

Explosive Pikes: Lie on your back on the incline bench, hold onto the bench above your head, and explosively kick your legs up toward the ceiling; lower your legs slowly to floor.

Lower Abdominal Medicine Ball Kicks: Lie on your back on the incline bench, hold onto the bench above your head, and explosively kick your legs out to kick a medicine ball to your partner; flex your legs before the next kick, keeping your legs up the entire time.

chapter 4 joint stability

Never believe you have insufficient time for the attention to detail that is essential to excellence. You have exactly the same twenty-four hours every day as Carl Lewis, Magic Johnson, and Evander Holyfield.

—Michael Colgan

BIOMECHANICS

Biomechanics is the study of the mechanics of the body. When we talk about our "mechanics," we're talking about the position of joints in relation to one another during movement. This is vital to us as athletes because as we discussed earlier, every movement we perform has what can be referred to as joint positions that are the most biomechanically advantageous. In other words, different activities have different ideal joint positions that allow us to move the most fluidly, efficiently, and powerfully. It is the job of our muscles and nervous system to be able to stabilize our joints in these different positions.

For example, imagine two people, Jane and John, with different lower-body biomechanics. When Jane stands on one leg and does a knee bend, her knee tracks optimally; in other words, her knee stays in line with her second toe (the toe next to her big toe). And, when Jane walks, her feet point straight ahead, and she also stretches every day. Now, let's say John's knees track over the inside of his big toe, his feet point slightly away from one another, and he never takes the time to stretch.

You happen to see Jane and John going for a run in your neighborhood one day. They're running side by side but with two very different strides. Jane seems to be striding effortlessly, almost floating as she runs. John, in contrast, looks labored, and his stride is awkward and too short for his leg length. His hamstrings are too tight to allow his heel to strike properly when he runs, and because his knees fall in and his toes point out, he has a very weak platform from which to propel himself forward. In other words, John's biomechanics result in a very inefficient stride. Moreover, just as Jane is starting to get warmed up, John is nearing exhaustion and ready to head home.

Can John improve his biomechanics and efficiency through crosstraining? Yes. He needs to start stretching on a regular basis, paying close attention to his glutes and hamstrings. His tight hamstrings limit his heel strike, and, like his hamstrings, his glutes are probably tight as well and partially responsible for his toes pointing outward. John can also improve the way his joints are aligned by training his nervous system how to recruit various muscles or joint stabilizers in the proper planes of movement.

KNEE TRACKING

The term *knee tracking* refers to the position of the patella or kneecap in relation to the foot during movement. This position is important because if the knee is tracking too far to one side or the other, it can place undue strain on the ankle, knee, and hip joints during movement, which in turn can ultimately result in an increased risk for injury and a loss of stability, strength, and power.

The most biomechanically advantageous knee-tracking position for most people is directly over the second toe. This position provides most of us with the best platform to maximize our strength and power. Deviations too far left or right of the optimal knee tracking position rely too heavily on tendons, ligaments, and muscle rather than bony structures as a base of support.

4.1

Ankle stability and foot structure play a large role in knee tracking. If your tendency is to *pronate,* or roll the foot and ankle inward, then your knee will more than likely follow. Conversely, if your tendency is to *supinate,* or roll your foot and ankle outward, then your knee will tend to track outward. Your goal is to try to maintain as neutral or evenly weighted a foot position as possible. Some athletic shoes are made to help correct for one tendency or the other. However, a more neutral foot position needs to become habitual or automatic because when you're performing any sport, that's the last thing you'll be thinking about!

Instability of the ankles, knees, or hips and lack of flexibility in any muscle of the lower body can also affect the way the knee tracks. For example, imbalances in strength or flexibility in the muscles of the hip joint can alter the position of the femur, which will directly affect the position of the knee.

FORCES

Every endurance sport requires that joints be able to withstand a variety of forces. For instance, our shoulders have to deal with rotational and linear forces when we pull water as we swim. Our ankles have to endure vibration and compression forces that travel up from our feet and down from our body weight when we run. Similarly, our knees need to withstand the fore and aft and vertical loads from pedal resistance and our body weight when we ride a bike.

The better our biomechanics, the more evenly these forces are dispersed through the soft tissue in our body. Ideal mechanics allow stresses to be absorbed and minimized by large muscles rather than connective tissue. Connective tissue such as small tendons and ligaments or the cartilage between our bones on joint surfaces is ill equipped to endure repetitive and significant rotational, compression, and other forces. When our biomechanics are poor, joint alignment is compromised, and we place a lot of stress on certain areas of a joint. Tendons and ligaments in our joints are then left to absorb forces greater than what they are designed for, and they become a vulnerable or weak part of the movement chain. Eventually these stresses may become too much for a particular tendon or ligament to handle, and we experience a breakdown in the form of an injury.

STABLE JOINTS

The rest of this chapter will discuss ways to help you develop more stable joints. Remember, a stable joint is less prone to injury and promotes balance and efficiency.

Joints are supported by tendons, ligaments, and muscles of varying sizes that work together in making small and gross adjustments depending on the type of movement we perform. For example, running requires stability of the ankle, knee, and hip joints as well as the pelvis and spine. Common injuries such as tears and strains of knee ligaments and ankle sprains could be avoided by improving lower-body flexibility as well as joint strength and stability.

The small muscles that surround our joints are referred to as *joint stabilizers*. This term helps distinguish them from the larger muscles in our body that are primarily responsible for movement. Joint stabilizers are located in ideal positions around a joint to help keep bones in position during movement and provide a solid platform from which our primary mover muscles can produce force.

For example, the deltoids are relatively small muscles that surround the shoulder joint. When we throw a ball, swing a golf club, do a push-up, swim, skate, or ski, we rely on these muscles to stabilize the shoulder joint and keep our upper arm centered in the joint. When the deltoids are stabilizing our shoulders optimally, we're able to utilize a higher percentage of the muscle fiber in our primary movers to swim or skate faster. When these joint stabilizers are weak or aren't recruited by our nervous system in the right amount at the right time during movement, our connective tissue has to take up the slack, resulting in a less stable platform for our primary movers.

THE NERVOUS SYSTEM

An important part of joint stability has to do with the nervous system. When our nervous system fails to recruit the right muscle in the right amount at the right time, our joint stabilizers are rendered ineffective. Ineffective joint stabilizers result in a loss of efficiency, a decrease in force production, and an increased risk for injury. When muscles responsible for joint stability aren't doing their job, a higher percentage of primary mover muscles are dedicated to help stabilize the joint. This leads to a decrease in both efficiency and force production because the primary mover musculature is distracted from doing what it does best. However, many primary movers don't attach at the locations necessary to stabilize the joint properly, and thus our risk for injury increases as connective tissue is overworked.

A fluid, efficient, and powerful stride, stroke, or skate results when the soft-tissue surrounding joints are coordinated by the nervous system to work in unison. It does us no good to have strong muscles if our nervous system isn't able to get those muscles to work in concert to stabilize our joints. In addition, the more stable a joint is, the less effort it takes to move and the more force we can produce with the same amount of effort during movement.

STRENGTHENING JOINT STABILIZERS

Joint stabilization training can be viewed as a combination of balance and strength training. Combining balance training with resistance training improves not only our strength but also joint and trunk stability. And, by forcing the body to recruit more stabilizing musculature, we integrate a higher percentage of our muscle mass and get a more effective and efficient workout.

It's important to point out the difference between traditional strength training and the strengthening of joint stabilizers. Traditional strength training involves greater resistance and more of an emphasis on strengthening large primary mover muscles. Joint stabilization training, in contrast, will require relatively little resistance and much more emphasis on training the nervous system to keep a joint or multiple joint in certain biomechanical positions during movement.

For instance, a classic bench press exercise requires very little joint stabilization. Your mass is supported by a bench, and the Olympic bar makes it relatively easy to keep the weight centered so that you can recruit a high percentage of your chest musculature. A dumbbell bench press requires a little more joint stability because each dumbbell needs to be stabilized to a greater degree. The dumbbell bench press doesn't allow you to work the chest musculature under as high a resistance load as the more stable bench press exercise. However, to truly challenge the nervous system to recruit the majority of shoulder joint stabilizers during movement, we would want to choose an exercise that was more unstable, such as doing push-ups on a balance board with one foot on the floor and one in the air. This method would obviously integrate trunk musculature, chest musculature, and joint stabilizers to work together and would force the nervous system to make continual adjustments during the push-up.

UPPER-BODY JOINT STABILITY EXERCISES

4.2 | Push-ups on Unstable Surface (such as two discs): With one hand on each disc, one foot on the floor, and the other foot in the air, maintain a neutral spine and level hips; perform this exercise slowly.

4.3 | Push-ups on Stability Ball: With your hands on the ball, one leg on the bench, and the other in the air, keep the ball centered as you push up; maintain a neutral spine and level hips; perform this exercise slowly.

4.4 | Single-Arm Dumbbell Bench Press While Bridging on Ball: With your feet on the floor and your shoulders and head supported by the ball, keep your hips up while pressing the dumbbell with one arm.

4.5 | Dumbbell Shoulder Internal and External Rotation: Relax your traps, keep a neutral spine, and keep your elbow at your side and arm bent at ninety degrees. Perform an internal rotation: rotate your arm toward the center of your body. Now perform an external rotation: rotate your arm away from the center of your body.

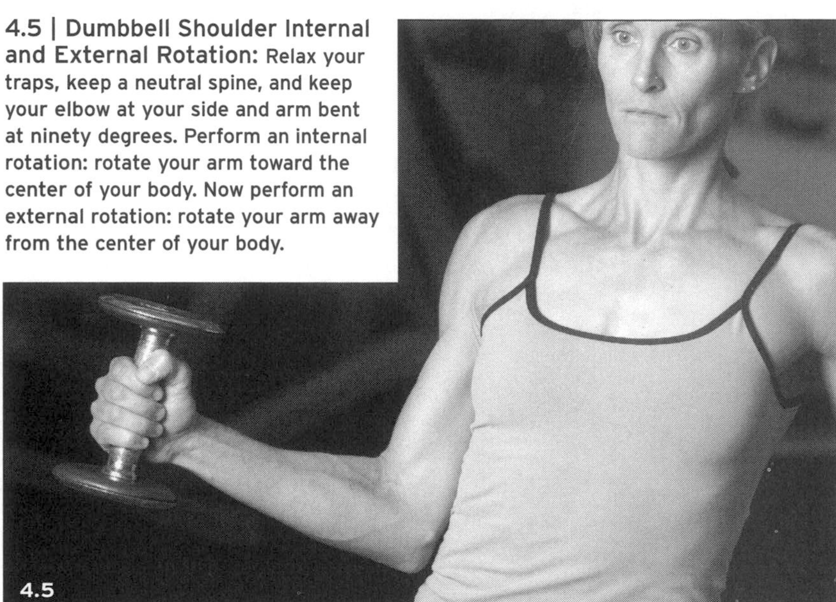

4.5

4.6

4.6 | Dumbbell Shoulder Raise in All Planes of Motion: With relaxed traps and your arm slightly bent, lift the dumbbell upward in various directions and angles.

4.7 | Single-Leg Bench Dip: Standing with one leg on the bench, slowly flex your knee, lowering your opposite foot toward the ground; maintain a neutral spine and level hips.

4.8 | Dynamic Hip and Glute Pull: Standing on one leg, extend slowly toward the cable, and pull the cable toward your hip with your opposite arm; maintain a neutral spine and level hips.

LOWER-BODY JOINT STABILITY EXERCISES

4.9 | Lateral Lunges onto Unstable Surface (such as a disc): Standing on either side of the disc, lunge sideways onto the disc with a neutral spine; stabilize, and then push back up to the starting position.

4.9

4.10

4.10 | Forward Lunge with Back Foot on Ball: Standing in a lunge position with your back foot on the stability ball, drop your hips slowly; stay centered with a neutral spine and level hips.

4.11

4.11 | Squats on Stability Ball: On your first attempt, place the ball in a squat cage, and have someone spot your hips while stabilizing the ball with one foot. Use the cage to lift yourself onto the ball; while holding onto the cage, lightly place your feet hip-width apart on the ball.

Squeeze the ball with your feet, and slowly drop down into a partial squat. Maintain a neutral spine with level hips, and look up. Do not let go of the cage until you are very comfortable staying centered on the ball.

With practice, you can eventually perform slow and controlled squats while standing on the stability ball. Always use a spotter, and stay in a sturdy squat cage that you can use to stabilize yourself instantaneously.

chapter 5
balance

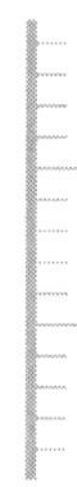

You only ever grow as a human being if you're outside your comfort zone.

—Percy Cerutty

So, what is a chapter on balance doing in a book geared toward endurance athletes? Well, we've examined flexibility, trunk stability, and joint stability. Balance can be viewed as a combination of all three of these elements or as overall stability. Good balance requires flexibility to maintain proper muscle length–tension relationships, trunk stability so that we can control our center of mass, and joint stability so that the right muscles are being recruited at the right time and in the right amount.

The two types of overall stability are static and dynamic balance. *Static balance* is your ability to stay centered in one place, such as standing on one leg without falling over. *Dynamic balance* refers to your ability to stabilize during movement. Both types of stability involve coordination of various muscles by your nervous system. The ability to stabilize statically is a precursor to dynamic stabilization. However, improving our dynamic balance is the most beneficial, functional, and sport-specific for any athlete.

DYNAMIC BALANCE

All sports require an element of dynamic balance (*dynamic*: constantly changing; *balance*: the ability to sustain or return the body's center of mass or line of gravity over its base of support). Consider the following quote from Michael Clark, the president of the National Academy of Sports Medicine: "Balance is a highly integrated and dynamic process that involves multiple neurological pathways. . . . For example, a relatively simple activity such as sprinting . . . requires losing and regaining your balance on one leg in less than one-tenth of a second." In other words, each running stride involves accelerating our mass, dynamically stabilizing our mass, and then decelerating our mass. And, like training our flexibility, trunk stability, and joint stability, increasing our overall stability will result in improved efficiency, force production, and injury prevention.

Swimming also requires the ability to stabilize dynamically as the trunk rotates and extremities propel us through the water. As a swimmer's overall stability or balance improves, he or she transfers more muscle energy to forward movement and loses less to the other planes of movement.

The more stable or balanced a cyclist is, the faster he or she will go as well. If we swerve or are unable to hold a straight line when we accelerate, climb, push a big gear, sprint, get out of the saddle, or assume an aerodynamic position, then we're losing speed. Or, if our lack of balance makes it difficult to take corners at high speed, then we're losing time to our competitors.

Have you ever ridden a bike on an indoor trainer that simply consists of two rolling drums and no support for you or your bike? Did it feel as if you were riding on ice at first? After a while your nervous system probably figured out how to dynamically stabilize or balance so that you could actually get a workout in without falling on your face. This is a form of balance training. Whether you noticed it or not, if you spent a lot of time on rollers, your stability on the road or on the trail also improved.

If you're in a sport such as mountain biking, in-line skating, or Nordic skiing, you already know how beneficial possessing good balance is to your sport. It's critical that mountain bikers be able to maintain their balance over uneven terrain, on steep descents, and whenever they need to shift their weight. In-line skaters and Nordic skiers feel a significant loss of speed and efficiency whenever they have to pause to regain their balance.

Improving our dynamic balance also helps us prevent the various injuries experienced by endurance sport athletes. The more balanced and centered we are during movement, the better we're able to disperse forces throughout the major muscles in the body. As we discussed in the chapter on joint stability, anything we can do to minimize the stress on connective tissue like tendons and ligaments, the healthier our joints will remain.

PROPRIOCEPTION

As with joint stability, our overall stability is very dependent on our nervous system. We have mechanoreceptors in the body that tell us the position and movement of limbs. The signals that the central nervous system receives from the numerous mechanoreceptors are referred to as *proprioception*.

Training proprioception is vital to endurance sport athletes because it is ultimately what will improve our dynamic balance. However, we must also be creative in finding new ways to challenge and stimulate our neurological pathways. We should continually strive to take our overall stability to a higher level. As with any type of training, our brain and muscles will eventually make adaptations in response to our proprioceptive training, and we'll have to up the ante and add variety in order to continue to make improvements.

We can train proprioception by simply integrating an element of instability in our training sessions—and not necessarily only in balance or joint stability workouts. We can also train proprioception to some extent during a strength workout, as we'll discuss in a later chapter. As a result, our workouts become more sport-specific as we challenge both the musculature and the nervous system to respond in a way that's similar to or greater than the demands of our sport.

BALANCE AND TRUNK STABILITY

Dynamic balance is dependent on trunk stability. *Trunk stability* is the ability to coordinate the muscles in the abdomen and back with specific movements. Since your center of gravity is below and behind your navel, the better you can stabilize your pelvis and spine, the better you'll be able to control the majority of your weight.

The point at which your spine meets your pelvis is essentially the largest joint in the body. In endurance sports, it's necessary to maintain a certain postural position and/or keep our hips and shoulders level in relation to one another in order to maximize efficiency. This creates a strong foundation for movement and makes it easier for joints such as our ankles, knees, hips, and shoulders to be stabilized.

Trunk musculature such as the transverse abdominis, internal obliques, external obliques, rectus abdominis, erector spinae, and latissimus dorsi all work together to stabilize the spine and pelvis. Thus, to reach your dynamic balance potential, you must also train your ability to stabilize your torso.

BALANCE AND JOINT STABILITY

Dynamic balance is also very dependent on joint stability. *Joint stability* refers in part to the integrity, flexibility, and strength of the muscles, tendons, and ligaments that provide movement for a joint. However, stability also requires the ability of our nervous system to recruit the right amounts from each muscle, large and small, to control movement of the joint.

If we can stabilize our trunk and joints quickly and effectively, we will more than likely have what we would call good balance. In endurance sports, it's important to develop full-body strength, flexibility, symmetry, and stability. As we discussed earlier, our trunk stability provides the foundation for movement. Stellar trunk strength and stability makes it easier for us to control the positions of our joints because it helps keep our center of gravity relatively quiet. However, if we're unable to keep our ankles from rolling inward and our knees from knocking, we'll probably have a tough time producing force.

Therefore, it's important to realize the effect that an unstable joint can have on our balance and consequently our performance. For example, a strained or sprained ligament in an ankle or knee will result in a less flexible, weaker, and less stable joint. This condition in turn can lead to a loss of symmetry between the left and right sides of our body, which will affect our ability to stabilize our mass and move fluidly and efficiently.

ATHLETIC STANCE

Balance starts with a strong *athletic stance*—your ready position that allows you to stay centered at all times. From this stance, you are ready for just about anything. This position should be relaxed and comfortable, allowing for the variety of movements your body will make.

An athletic stance varies somewhat from individual to individual. However, almost everyone's body position should include feet hip- to shoulder-width apart; more weight on the balls of the feet; a bend in the ankles and knees; a slight drop in the hips; chest up with a natural and slightly forward spine position; hands out in front, with elbows slightly bent; relaxed shoulders; and head level to the ground to allow eyes to look ahead.

The athletic stance should be used when you're training your balance and can be found by jumping up in the air with your eyes closed a few times. Each time you land, take note of the position your body naturally relaxes into. Try to find that position more quickly with every jump. After a few jumps, open your eyes and analyze your stance. You should feel light on your feet, with your center of gravity low, balanced, and ready to move in any direction.

BALANCE TRAINING

The beauty of balance training is that you can do many of these exercises several times a week without ever really feeling fatigued. For example, many athletes in dynamic balance sports will train their balance in fifteen- to thirty-minute workouts three to four times per week. Oftentimes, athletes will train balance and agility in the same workout on days that they aren't strength training. And, since these workouts don't need to be very strenuous, they can be done on a recovery day or the day before a hard workout or competition.

As we've discussed, you'll find it easier to balance if you maintain an athletic stance and use your trunk musculature. It's also helpful to focus your eyes on a point at least a few feet in front of you and at eye level to keep your head up. The following exercises should be done in a safe area and only after a good warmup and a light stretch.

STATIC BALANCE EXERCISES

5.1 | Balls of Feet on Edge of Step with Eyes Closed: **Stand with your feet hip-width apart and the balls of both feet on the edge of a step; keep a slight bend in your knees, and once centered, close your eyes to increase the difficulty.**

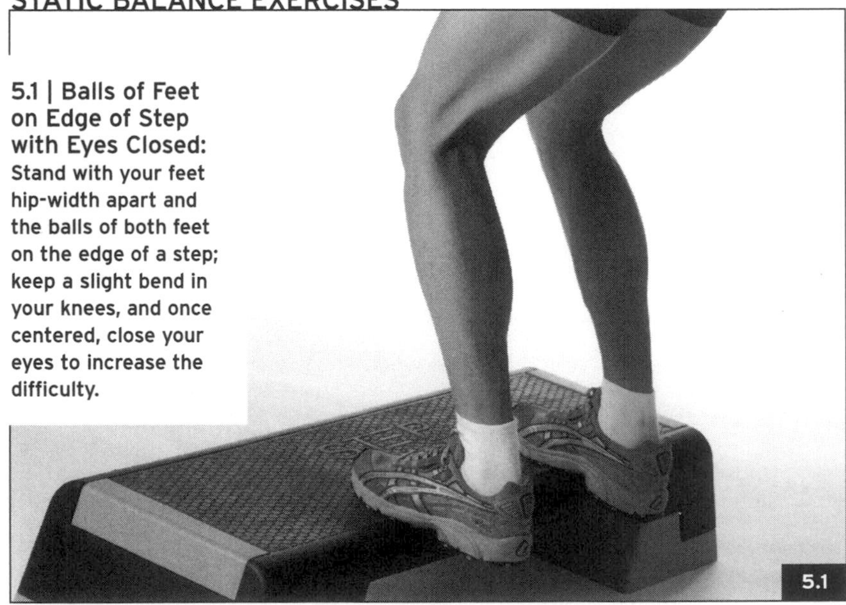

5.1

5.2 | Heels of Feet on Edge of Step with Eyes Closed: Stand with your feet hip-width apart; with the heels of both feet on the edge of a step, keep a slight bend in your knees, and, once centered, close your eyes to increase the difficulty.

5.2

5.3 | Reaching Down and Rotating Back on One Leg on Unstable Surface: While standing on disc with one leg, reach down with both hands toward your foot, reach back and rotate overhead, and then reach down and rotate back to the other side, all while staying as stable as possible.

5.3

5.4 | Reaching and Rotating While Standing on One Leg on Unstable Surface (such as a disc): While standing on a disc on one leg, with your arms out to both sides, rotate to touch one toe; come back to the center, and rotate down with your opposite hand, keeping both arms straight, a neutral spine, and a slight bend in your knee.

5.5 | Partner Tug-of-War Standing on One Leg on Unstable Surface (such as half foam rolls): Stand on a half foam roll with a slight bend in your knee and level hips and shoulders; have your partner do the same a few feet away. Both you and your partner hold ends of a rope and try to pull each other off balance; the rope can slide through your hands, but neither person can let go of the rope.

DYNAMIC BALANCE EXERCISES

5.6

5.6 | Unstable Surface Obstacle Course: Arrange a series of unstable objects such as discs, foam rolls, and half foam rolls, varying the distance between objects from short steps to long steps to short hops to big jumps. Negotiate through the obstacle course slowly at first, trying to stay as centered as possible; once you've mastered the course, rearrange the objects or go through the course faster to increase difficulty.

Walking on Narrow Beam, Railing, or Tightrope: Look ahead, focusing on a stabilizing center of mass, keeping your hips and shoulders level.

5.7

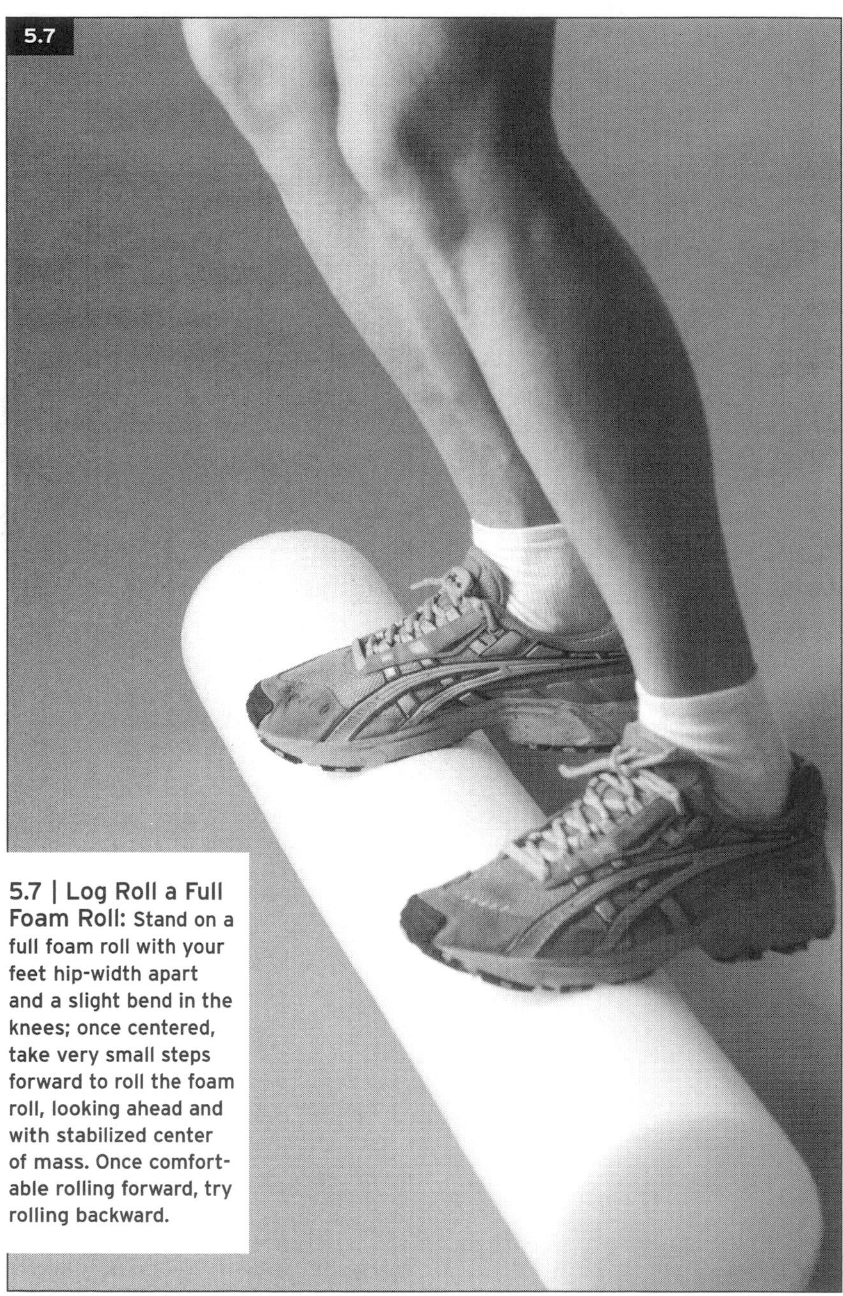

5.7 | Log Roll a Full Foam Roll: Stand on a full foam roll with your feet hip-width apart and a slight bend in the knees; once centered, take very small steps forward to roll the foam roll, looking ahead and with stabilized center of mass. Once comfortable rolling forward, try rolling backward.

5.8 | Squat on Balance Board While Throwing Medicine Ball to Partner: Stand on a balance board with your feet hip-width apart and a slight bend in the knees. Once centered, have your partner throw the medicine ball, catch it, stabilize, squat down, stand up, and throw the ball back to your partner without falling off the board. Once comfortable, try throwing a heavier ball or a lighter ball with one arm at various angles; this variation requires a high degree of proficiency in standing on the balance board.

Squat on Stability Ball While Throwing Medicine Ball to Partner: Stand on a stability ball with your feet hip-width apart and a slight bend in the knees. Once centered, have your partner throw the medicine ball, catch it, stabilize, squat down, stand up, and throw the ball back to your partner without falling off the ball. Once comfortable, try throwing a heavier ball or a lighter ball with one arm at various angles; this variation requires a high degree of proficiency in standing on the stability ball.

DYNAMIC BALANCE STRENGTH TRAINING

Once you've mastered a dynamic balance exercise, one way to increase the difficulty is to introduce a strength component. For example, when standing on a balance board becomes easy, you can grab a couple of dumbbells and do arm curls while you're balancing. As a result, one exercise can integrate and improve dynamic balance, trunk stabilization, and strength.

Athletes at every level can also benefit greatly from squatting on an unstable surface. For instance, doing squats to a ninety-degree bend in the knees while standing on a stability ball is a great exercise to improve the strength and stability of the ankles, knees, hips, and trunk. When this exercise becomes easy, you can take it to another level by holding or throwing a medicine ball or wearing a weighted vest. This is the ultimate in sport-specific training and is essential for any athlete who wants to take performance to the next level.

Crosstraining Activities to Train Dynamic Balance

In-line skating	*Surfing*
Ice skating	*Water skiing*
Alpine skiing	*Wakeboarding*
Nordic skiing	*Skateboarding*
Snowboarding	*Kayaking*

VARIETY

It's important to have a lot of variety in the types of balance exercises you perform. As with anything, the body—more specifically, the nervous system—will adapt to a particular movement or direction of instability. To progress, you must continually challenge your ability to balance dynamically with new and more difficult exercises. You'll find that once you've done an exercise for a while, your body will adapt, becoming very efficient and quickly making the adjustments necessary to keep you centered. If you continuously vary the exercises slightly and introduce more instability, you not only will make bigger improvements in your ability to dynamically stabilize but will also keep the workouts fun and thus do them more often.

chapter 6
agility

Things may come to those who wait. But only the things left behind by those who hustle. —Abraham Lincoln

IMBALANCES

We've discussed how muscle imbalances can affect our performance. We understand the importance of maintaining flexibility and strength symmetry between the front and back and left and right sides of our body. However, there's another aspect of strength and conditioning that endurance sport athletes tend to ignore: their overall athleticism. An important part of our overall athleticism is our speed, quickness, and coordination, otherwise known as *agility*.

There are three planes of movement. Imagine dividing the body in half three different ways. The *frontal* plane can be found by drawing an imaginary line to divide the body into anterior (front) and posterior (back) halves. The *sagittal* plane can be viewed by drawing an imaginary line between the right and left sides of the body. The *transverse* plane can be seen by drawing an imaginary line between the top and bottom halves of the body.

Because endurance sports are measured by a clock, we're concerned with forward progress. As a result, we spend the vast majority of our exercising time moving in the frontal plane. By ignoring the other two planes of movement, though, we become imbalanced. In time, our quickness, speed, and coordination in the other two planes of movement can deteriorate to the point where performance in our sport decreases and risk for injury increases.

As we've discussed in previous chapters, it's important to maintain muscular balance and correct posture. One way to do this is to incorporate side-to-side and rotational movements into our training programs. When we're strong in all three planes of movement, we develop more power and efficiency in any one plane because we become more balanced and stable.

ATHLETICISM AND PERFORMANCE

How does improving overall athleticism improve performance? Through focused, effective, and relevant crosstraining exercises, we can stimulate our nervous system to learn how to recruit muscles more quickly and to a greater extent than we ask them to be utilized during our sport. In other words, we can train beyond the demands of our sport and create more beneficial neurological and physiological adaptations through crosstraining.

Other benefits result from improving our overall athleticism and preventing speed, quickness, and coordination imbalances in other planes of movement. When our nervous system and musculature is able to react quickly in the sagittal and transverse planes of movement to make small adjustments in joint position due to differences in things like terrain, wind, currents, and competitor positions, we become more efficient. When we're slow to react to these forces or challenges, we lose speed, time, and energy getting back on track or into our rhythm.

ATHLETICISM AND INJURY PREVENTION

When we train to improve our overall athleticism, we're also helping prevent injury. The more accustomed our nervous system and musculature is to performing in and stabilizing us in other planes of movement, the more quickly we can react in all situations. This means that we will be better able to recover from slips, trips, stumbles, or anything else that puts us in unforeseen and potentially injury-causing positions.

For example, let's say a triathlete is halfway through his open-water swim and is surrounded by several other competitors. He suddenly encounters an entanglement of slow or stopped swimmers at the turnaround point. A swimmer who hasn't ignored the importance of maintaining overall athleticism might be able to react quickly and make the adjustments needed in order to avoid being kicked or elbowed in the arm, face, or shoulder. A not-so-agile swimmer might have to endure a muscle contusion or worse for the rest of the race!

AGILITY'S ROLE IN PERFORMANCE

The two components of agility are coordination and speed. As we know, the faster we attempt to perform a movement, the less precise we become. However, if we train correctly, we can improve our agility. We can create adaptations in our nervous system and musculature by performing drills that will increase accuracy at higher speeds. This will directly translate to greater agility in everything we do.

Agility is an essential element of our endurance sport performance. Many of the movements we make in our feet, ankles, knees, hips, and shoulders happen with a great deal of precision and speed. As with any sport, we need to contract a number of small and large muscles surrounding each joint that's involved in a movement, in varying amounts. These muscles are recruited by our nervous system in response to factors such as speed changes, gravitational forces, water resistance, and terrain changes. We make constant adjustments in this muscle recruitment throughout a training session or race. When done well, our technique looks fluid, powerful, and athletic.

We must be agile or precise in our weight distribution so as not to overcompensate in reaction to forces that are exerted on us. Consider the analogy of driving on a dirt road or on ice. If you take a corner too fast and the back end begins to slide, you want to turn the steering wheel in the direction of the skid. However, you only want to turn it as much as you need to get the vehicle back to center. If you overreact and turn the wheel too much, you'll send the back end sliding in the opposite direction. Similarly, when we make small adjustments to joints all the way from our feet to our neck, we need a multitude of muscles to coordinate their contractions very quickly, in just the right amount, in order to execute the desired movement.

As we discussed earlier, it's important that we develop speed and accuracy in *all* planes of movement. This will result in the greatest gains in agility and hence do the most to maintain our overall athleticism.

Because our time and energy are limited, as endurance athletes, we obviously wouldn't dedicate as much training time to developing agility as, say, a soccer player would. However, our swimming, running, cycling, and skating techniques are learned skills just as proper kicking, dribbling, and passing techniques are in soccer. As such, the more agility we can maintain in all planes of movement, the more efficient we'll become in the movement patterns that we've developed in our sport. For example, if a tennis player can develop the coordination, speed, quickness, accuracy, and stability to hit a forehand on the run, her nervous system and musculature will find it that much easier to efficiently hit a forehand while standing on the baseline. Similarly, if we can move fluidly, efficiently, powerfully, and accurately in all planes of movement with our joints in various positions, our nervous system and musculature will develop even more proficiency in our repetitive and established movement patterns.

CARDIOVASCULAR DEMANDS

Cardiovascular fitness refers to how accustomed your heart and lungs are to exercise. This is important because working muscles require oxygen to contract effectively. Muscles that work better help us increase safety, enjoyment, and performance. This element of fitness is essential as it is the foundation for endurance, strength, power, stability, and agility development. If you think of your overall fitness as a pyramid, cardiovascular exercise would be the broad base. Without such a foundation, you'll be unable to build your conditioning pyramid to its maximal potential.

The two main types of cardiovascular exercise are aerobic and anaerobic. *Aerobic* exercise is physical activity performed at an intensity in which your heart and lungs are able to deliver adequate oxygen to working muscles. The primary energy source of prolonged aerobic efforts is fat. *Anaerobic* exercise is physical activity in which your heart and lungs are unable to meet the oxygen demands of the musculature involved. Because fat can only be "burned" in the presence of oxygen, the primary energy source of anaerobic activity is glycogen. Glycogen is the storage carbohydrate that's unique to mammals. The largest reserves of this energy source can be found in our muscles, making it a readily available fuel.

AEROBIC CAPACITY

Aerobic capacity refers to a person's ability to sustain a medium intensity aerobic effort for extended periods of time. Developing a high capacity for aerobic activity means that your lungs get a good deal of oxygen into the bloodstream quickly and that your heart is effective at pumping this oxygenated blood to working muscles. As an endurance athlete, you know that increasing aerobic capacity is the first step in developing overall fitness. A high aerobic capacity will improve endurance and is required to achieve better anaerobic endurance.

How to Improve

Aerobic capacity can be improved through prolonged, medium-intensity aerobic activity. Aerobic workouts should last at least thirty minutes and be performed above 55 percent of your maximum heart rate and below your anaerobic threshold.

A common formula for calculating your maximum heart rate is to subtract your age from 220. This method doesn't hold true, however, for a lot of experienced endurance athletes. Their maximum heart rate is usually higher than the number they would get by using this equation. However, it can give you a ballpark number that will work for estimating where your heart rate should be for aerobic and anaerobic workouts.

You can also find your maximum heart rate by wearing a heart rate monitor during a hill sprint workout. For example, after a ten- to thirty-minute warmup, find a steep hill to run up. If you were to run as fast as you can up that hill for ten to fifteen seconds and walk down, your maximum heart rate should register two to three seconds after you finish the fourth or fifth sprint. Such a heart rate test is very strenuous, however, and should only be attempted by well-conditioned athletes.

The *anaerobic threshold* (AT) is the point at which the muscles go into oxygen debt and lactic acid, the by-product of metabolizing glycogen, is produced more quickly than it can be cleared from working muscles. As a result, lactic acid concentration increases and creates an acidic environment that makes it difficult for the muscle to contract. This is also the point at which working muscles and lung musculature will start to feel as if they're "burning" and fatigue quickly. Exercise performed above the anaerobic threshold results in improving *lactate tolerance* (LT), or the ability for working muscles to contract in a more acidic environment. This type of exercise will also train the body to adapt to the stress by becoming more efficient at clearing lactic acid from working muscles.

The anaerobic threshold for most avid exercisers is reached between 80 and 90 percent of their maximum heart rate (see Table 6.1). For example, if an active person's max is 200 beats per minute (bpm) then his AT will probably be somewhere between 160 and 180. You'll probably feel this same "burn" after you've been running at a comfortable, relaxed pace on flat ground for a while and then attempt to maintain the same speed up a hill. This is your anaerobic threshold, and if you were wearing a heart rate monitor, you'd find that your heart rate would be between 80 and 90 percent of your maximum heart rate. Thus, aerobic activity meant to improve aerobic capacity should be performed below this point, at a heart rate between 55 and 80 percent of your maximum heart rate.

TABLE 6.1 Heart Rate Zones Correlating to Aerobic and Anaerobic Workouts

HEART RATE ZONE	WORKOUTS
55%-70% of your maximum heart rate	Long aerobic workouts to improve endurance
71%-83% of your maximum heart rate	Aerobic intervals to improve anaerobic threshold
84%-92% of your maximum heart rate	Anaerobic intervals to improve lactate threshold
93%-97% of your maximum heart rate	Anaerobic work to improve maximal oxygen uptake
98%-100% of your maximum heart rate	Sprint workouts to improve maximal efforts

AEROBIC INTERVAL TRAINING

Interval training is a type of energy system workout that involves periods of intensity followed by rest. It allows more work to be performed at higher exercise intensities with the same or less fatigue as continuous training. Interval training can be done while performing virtually any aerobic activity, including, of course, your particular endurance sport.

Aerobic intervals are relatively painless and are most effective when done between five and ten beats per minute below the anaerobic threshold. As we discussed before, the AT for most active people is between 80 and 90 percent of their maximum heart rate. It's better to err on the side of a little too easy than a little too hard. After all, once you've reached AT, you're no longer training to increase

Aerobic Intervals

This type of interval training will help increase your anaerobic threshold. Having a high anaerobic threshold will allow you to go relatively hard for extended periods of time before going into oxygen debt. As a result, you'll be able to recover more quickly between efforts and have more energetic workout sessions.

TABLE 6.2 Example of a Relatively Easy **30-Minute Aerobic** Interval Session

ACTIVITY	INTENSITY	HEART RATE
10-minute warmup	Low	55%–65% of max
1.5-minute aerobic interval	Medium	5–10 bpm below AT
2-minute recovery	Low	55%–65% of max
2-minute aerobic interval	Medium	5–10 bpm below AT
3-minute recovery	Low	55%–65% of max
1.5-minute aerobic interval	Medium	5–10 bpm below AT
10-minute cooldown	Low	55%–65% of max

TABLE 6.3 Example of a More Difficult **60-minute Aerobic** Interval Session

ACTIVITY	INTENSITY	HEART RATE
15-minute warmup	Low	55%–65% of max
4-minute aerobic interval	Medium	5–10 bpm below AT
4-minute recovery	Low	55%–65% of max
5-minute aerobic interval	Medium	5–10 bpm below AT
4-minute recovery	Low	55%–65% of max
5-minute aerobic interval	Medium	5–10 bpm below AT
4-minute recovery	Low	55%–65% of max
4-minute aerobic interval	Medium	5–10 bpm below AT
15-minute cooldown	Low	55%–65% of max

the threshold but are training muscle lactate tolerance, or your muscle's ability to contract in a more acidic environment. In other words, if you've reached the point of lung and muscle burn, you've gone too hard.

Aerobic interval sessions should last from thirty to sixty minutes total, with individual intervals lasting from one to ten minutes and rest of three to six minutes in between. Tables 6.2 and 6.3 present examples of thirty- and sixty-minute interval sessions.

ANAEROBIC ENDURANCE

Anaerobic endurance refers to a person's ability to sustain a high-intensity anaerobic effort for relatively short periods of time. For example, the 100- and 400-meter track events in running utilize the anaerobic energy system, whereas a marathon primarily makes use of the aerobic energy system. In other words, someone with good anaerobic endurance is able to utilize glycogen as an energy source efficiently, and his or her muscles are trained to contract in a more acidic environment.

ANAEROBIC INTERVAL TRAINING

Anaerobic interval training will help increase muscle lactate tolerance. As a result, working muscles will be able to contract in a more acidic environment and won't fatigue as quickly. Anaerobic intervals are shorter and more painful than aerobic intervals. These intervals are done above the AT and are accompanied by a great deal of lung and muscle burn. An anaerobic interval session might also last from thirty to sixty minutes. Each interval might be thirty seconds to two minutes in length, with one to five minutes of rest in between. Tables 6.4 and 6.5 describe examples of thirty- and sixty-minute anaerobic interval workouts.

Another type of anaerobic interval training is a sprint workout. Sprint workouts consist of very short, all-out intervals. Such training is designed to overload an athlete or to improve the athlete's ability to give maximal efforts and recover between them. Sprints utilize the adenosine triphosphate–creatine phosphate

TABLE 6.4 Example of a Relatively Easy **30-Minute Anaerobic** Interval Session

ACTIVITY	INTENSITY	HEART RATE
10-minute warmup	Low	55%-65% of max
1-minute anaerobic interval	High	Above AT
3-minute recovery	Low	55%-65% of max
1-minute anaerobic interval	High	Above AT
4-minute recovery	Low	55%-65% of max
1-minute anaerobic interval	High	Above AT
10-minute cooldown	Low	55%-65% of max

TABLE 6.5 Example of a More Difficult **60-Minute Anaerobic** Interval Session

ACTIVITY	INTENSITY	HEART RATE
20-minute warmup	Low	55%-65% of max
45-second anaerobic interval	High	Above AT
90-second recovery	Low	55%-65% of max
1-minute anaerobic interval	High	Above AT
3-minute recovery	Low	55%-65% of max
1-minute anaerobic interval	High	Above AT
4-minute recovery	Low	55%-65% of max
1-minute anaerobic interval	High	Above AT
3-minute recovery	Low	55%-65% of max
1-minute anaerobic interval	High	Above AT
3-minute recovery	Low	55%-65% of max
45-second anaerobic interval	High	Above AT
20-minute cooldown	Low	55%-65% of max

(ATP-CP) energy system. This is an energy source that can be utilized very rapidly by working muscles but is also in very limited supply. As a result, each sprint should last about ten seconds and should be followed by two to five minutes of rest depending on your goal. Since a sprint workout is effectively over once you're unable to get your heart rate well above your anaerobic threshold, five to ten sprints should suffice. Sprint workouts are very strenuous, specialized workouts that should only be attempted after an athlete is very well conditioned.

The workouts described here are very structured and will be most effective when performed with the use of a heart rate monitor. However, if you're pretty in tune with your body and have a good sense of how hard your heart and lungs are working, you can also go by feel.

As with any physical activity, it's important to ease yourself into interval training. Start with very short intervals and a lot of rest, and then gradually progress. Because it's easy to burn out both physically and mentally on this type of training program, make sure you've thought through when it fits within your program.

Agility workouts can also be designed to double as an interval workout. For example, you can perform a drill for a set period of time and then give yourself just enough rest to perform the next drill at full intensity again but not so much rest that your heart rate drops below zone 1.

DRILLS

Any drill to improve quickness and agility should be functional. In other words, you should be able to relate it to movements and performance in your sport whenever possible. This is relatively easy because most sports are so dynamic that we need to train virtually every muscle in our body to help us become more agile. I have given you some examples of agility drills that I use, but I urge you to do some brainstorming of your own. It's been my experience that athletes are more apt to enjoy agility training if they play a role in creating the workouts.

You should consider numerous variables when developing agility drills. I don't expect every drill you come up with to be entirely sport-specific. The idea is that, as I've mentioned throughout this book, you critically think about what and why you're doing something in an effort to get the best possible results. The objective is to train your body to be prepared beyond the demands placed on you by your sport, while still keeping things relatively safe. We want to perform drills as quickly and accurately as possible while also promoting proper body positions and biomechanics.

AGILITY DRILLS

6.1 | **Quick Feet Crossover:** Stand with your feet hip-width apart over a line on the ground. Cross your feet over the line and back; then cross your feet the opposite way and back. Once comfortable, repeat at a faster rate. To measure your progress, record how many crossovers you complete in a set time. Keep a slight bend in the knees, look ahead, be accurate, and stay light on your feet.

6.2 | **Quick Feet Step-ups:** Standing facing a step, alternate stepping onto the step with one foot and then the other. Once comfortable, repeat at a faster rate. To measure your progress, record how many step-ups you complete in a given amount of time. Look ahead, be accurate, and stay light on your feet.

6.3 | Agility Ladder: Lay the agility ladder flat on the ground, and perform various movements stepping or hopping in and out of the squares laterally and fore-aft with one leg, two legs, or alternating legs. Look ahead, be accurate, and stay light on your feet.

6.4 | Hexagonal Drill: Lay tape on the ground in the shape of a hexagon. Hop in and out of the hexagon at each of its sides. Perform this drill clockwise, counterclockwise, laterally, and fore-aft. To measure your progress, record how long it takes to get through the hexagon. Look ahead, be accurate, and stay light on your feet.

Boulder Drill: Find an area that has several boulders of varying sizes and shapes close to each other. Create an agility course by walking slowly through the boulders and placing brightly colored tape at spots where you step. Negotiate the course you've created. As you become more comfortable and know where the course goes, increase your speed. To measure your progress, record how long it takes to get through the course. Look ahead, be accurate, and stay light on your feet.

Agility Drill Variables that Can Be Manipulated

1. The length of the particular drill as well as the duration of the workout. Quickness and agility won't improve if you're fatigued. Each drill should be relatively short, ten to thirty seconds, and the whole workout should take between twenty and sixty minutes.

2. Incorporation of all three planes of movement. Develop drills that make you move in all directions: lateral, rotational, flexion, extension, and a combination of these planes.

3. Variation of the drills in your workouts. As with anything, your body will adapt to specific movements; you thus need to continually challenge your musculature and nervous system by changing things up.

4. The range of motion required of the drill. Since our sports are dynamic, the range of motion required during a drill should also be dynamic.

5. The limbs, muscles, and joints involved. Sport specificity in this area means a higher likelihood of the drill improving our performance.

6. The muscle contraction required. For example, our legs contract both concentrically and eccentrically when we run, swim, ride, and skate; concentrically when we extend our legs; and eccentrically when we flex our knees.

7. The coordination of body parts during a drill. You'll want to keep your upper body stable and quiet during certain drills that involve you being quick with your feet, ankles, knees, and hips.

8. The intensity of the movement. For example, a drill requiring you to hop on one leg is more intense than the same drill done while hopping on both legs at the same time.

9. The perceptual skills incorporated into your drills. Some of your drills should incorporate and challenge your ability to assess and react to different variables.

10. The energy system demands incorporated into your agility workouts. Certain exercises should place a similar demand on your heart and lungs as your sport does.

Agility Drill Equipment Ideas

1. ***Jump rope***—great for warming up and can be used as an agility drill by forcing you to jump precisely over a line or into squares drawn on the ground with chalk or created with masking tape

2. ***Agility ladder***—a ladder made usually of plastic and nylon and placed flat on the ground; can be used for a multitude of different one- and two-legged jumping, hopping, or quick-stepping drills

3. ***Hurdles***—usually made of plastic and vary in height from six to eighteen inches; can be used for various one- and two-legged jumping or hopping drills alone or in conjunction with agility ladder

4. ***Cones***—varied in height and can be used for a multitude of different one- and two-legged jumping, hopping, quick-stepping, or running drills

5. ***Tape***—great for making different length lines or shapes on the ground that you have to jump or step over or into with one or two legs

6. ***Boxes of varying heights that can support your weight***—usually referred to as plyometric boxes; can be used for a multitude of different one- and two-legged jumping, hopping, or quick-stepping drills alone or used with other boxes

7. ***Full foam rolls***—dense, Styrofoam rolls that you can roll forward or backward like a log; promote fast feet and are great for challenging the small, fast-twitch muscle fibers in the foot and ankle

8. ***Hackisack***—small beanbags you can juggle with anything but your hands; great for promoting eye-foot coordination and fast reactions; most fun used with two or three other people

9. ***Reaction ball***—small, rubber, odd-shaped balls that bounce unpredictably when thrown on hard surfaces; great for improving reaction times and overall quickness and agility

10. ***Medicine ball***—a heavy ball that you can use to increase the difficulty of almost any agility and quickness drill; can hold the ball in front of you to promote a quiet upper body or play catch with someone else while your feet are performing a particular drill

CROSSTRAINING

Although structured agility workouts are extremely effective, we can also train these elements through certain crosstraining activities. Agility crosstraining helps keep us from getting burned out on the drills we've created and can just be plain fun!

How do we incorporate agility training into our overall training program? As mentioned earlier, agility training doesn't need to take up very much of your overall training time. Perhaps you'll find it necessary to devote thirty to sixty minutes per week to developing agility in the off-season and maybe only fifteen to thirty minutes per week during the season. You can incorporate some speed and accuracy drills into other workouts or do some aerobic crosstraining in the off-season by playing a game like soccer. As with all crosstraining, you'll need to determine what your individual goals, needs, wants, and abilities are to make an informed decision as to how much and what kind of agility training you should be doing. And, if you're able to keep your agility training varied, fun, and effective, it will always be time and energy well spent.

Agility Crosstraining Activities

Alpine skiing
Basketball
Beach volleyball
Football
In-line skating
Racquetball
Skateboarding
Soccer
Tennis
Ultimate Frisbee
Training agility

chapter 7 strength

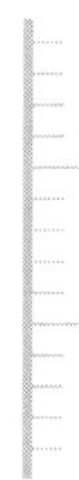

Fatigue makes cowards of us all. —*Vince Lombardi*

BODY COMPOSITION

As endurance athletes, we're concerned with our weight. If we weigh more, it takes more energy to propel us forward. However, it's very important that we distinguish between movable mass such as muscle and dead weight such as fat. Our *body mass*, or what we weigh, is directly related to our body composition. *Body composition* refers to the percentages of our mass that are made up of things like bone, organs, fat, muscle, and other soft tissue.

We can affect our mass by gaining or losing fat and lean muscle through changes in diet and exercise. Overall, our ideal total weight will be determined not only by the percentage of body fat and lean muscle mass but by height, weight, age, gender, activity level, and the type of physical activity we perform. Muscle is denser than fat and therefore weighs more. For example, a person could lose a significant amount of body fat, gain some muscle mass, and still weigh the same. Thus, knowing a person's weight alone isn't a great indicator of fitness. It's more important to determine an endurance athlete's body fat and lean muscle mass percentages.

Nonathletes tend to strive to lower their percentage of body fat for aesthetic reasons, which in turn can improve self-confidence. There are also obvious functional reasons to having a percentage of body fat within a "normal" range. If your body fat levels are high, then losing fat will minimize the amount of dead weight resisting you when you exercise, decrease stress on your heart, increase your energy levels, and improve your range of motion when you're moving. However, having too low a body fat percentage can decrease energy levels, the ability to recover from an injury, and our immune response, and it can inhibit all sorts of physiological processes.

Body fat percentage is the percentage of total body mass that consists of fat. Normal body fat percentages range from 5 to 15 percent for males and 15 to 25 percent for females. The low end of the spectrum is reserved for serious athletes or individuals with unique genetics. It should be noted that a person's optimal body fat percentage is extremely individual and will be influenced by factors such as age, activity level, activity type, genetics, and percentage of lean muscle mass.

Lean muscle mass percentage is the percentage of total weight that is made up of muscle. Increasing our muscle mass will help us raise our metabolism, which will then make it easier to manage our body fat percentage.

Body composition can be determined in numerous ways. The most common, easily accessible, and inexpensive techniques are skin fold measurements and electric current analyzers. Skin fold measurements involve the use of calipers to pinch the skin in certain areas of the body. Electric current analyzers use electrodes placed on the hands and feet to measure the amount of resistance encountered between the two sites. The results for both methods are then calculated taking into consideration a person's age, gender, height, weight, and activity level.

If you're interested in seeking out either of these methods for determining body composition, you should do a little research of your own. Most health clubs and physical therapy offices have calipers to take skin fold measurements. However, results can vary significantly depending on who's taking the measurements and the sites on the body used to take measurements. Some health clubs, physical therapy offices, and university human performance labs have electric current analyzers. For either method, consistency is the key. Be sure to ask for the most qualified personnel at a particular facility, and try to seek out the same person the next time you want to get tested.

A more expensive and accurate method for analyzing body composition is hydrostatic weighing. This technique is usually done in a university laboratory, research facility, or private physical performance institute that offers lab testing for athletes. It involves submerging the subject in a tank of water. Because fat tends to float and muscle sinks, the weighing device can determine body composition more precisely.

THE MYTH

For decades, many athletes and coaches in a variety of sports rejected the idea of strength training. In fact, many dismissed the need for any type of crosstraining. However, we now know that athletes in every sport can enhance their performance by improving sport-specific fitness, balance, agility, quickness, speed, power, and strength through individualized crosstraining workouts.

It's widely accepted that attempting to gain fitness by only performing your specific sport, for hours on end, can lead to fatigue, which in turn can result in overuse injuries, unwanted biomechanical habits, and mental burnout. As an athlete becomes fatigued, he or she is unable to stabilize joints properly, which can lead to chronic injuries. Moreover, when athletes in endurance sports train only their sport excessively, it's common to see breakdowns in technique that then lead to a decrease in performance. This is because as the primary musculature you use in your sport gets tired, you'll begin to recruit other muscles or adopt unusual body positions to compensate. The real killer is that it takes considerably more repetitions to correct a faulty movement pattern than it did to learn the movement correctly the first time. Finally, resistance training helps us stay sharp not only physically but also mentally. It's common to see athletes who have very little diversity in their training programs burn out much more quickly than those who crosstrain.

A vast majority of athletes in all sports incorporate some type of strength and power training into their programs. However, when you mention strength and power development to many endurance athletes, they still think football or bodybuilding. We need to realize the difference between traditional strength training and functional strength training.

FUNCTIONAL STRENGTH

Resistance training with the goal of developing functional strength is much different than what you see most muscle-bound lifters in the weight room doing. I often hear endurance athletes express concern about going to the gym because they fear putting on muscle mass. It is common knowledge and simple physics that excess weight can slow us down. However, what most of us fail to recognize is that even body types that can build mass very easily can strength train without gaining weight. That's right. It's possible to make gains in strength without significantly increasing the size of our muscles. In addition, it's difficult to build muscle mass when you are also doing a lot of cardiovascular training.

Many of us just haven't been exposed to the ways we can enhance performance through strength training. The frequency of workouts, the amount of weight that's lifted, the type of motion of the exercise, the tempo at which it's performed, and the number of sets and repetitions in the workout all will affect the time that a muscle is put under tension. The time a muscle is under tension will affect how the body adapts to the stresses it's confronted with.

For instance, how many avid rock climbers have you seen that look like bodybuilders or football players? Rock climbers are constantly defying gravity, and consequently their muscles spend a lot of time under tension. However, since they use several muscles to perform each move, the load placed on any specific muscle is relatively low. The vast majority of rock climbers have a high strength-to-weight ratio and possess lean muscle mass without putting on excess weight. This is because *hypertrophy*, or growing the size of a muscle, is an adaptation that our bodies make in response to stress. If you load a muscle maximally day after day, your body will eventually grow the muscle in an effort to meet those demands.

When we train functionally, we train *movements* as opposed to just muscles, which places a moderate load on any one muscle. Functional resistance training involves more joints and muscles per exercise than conventional fixed machine strength training. We also integrate numerous trunk and joint stabilizers as opposed to trying to work a muscle in isolation. And, because our goal is to improve function, our strength training workouts are full body, short in duration, and followed by adequate recovery. As a result, functional resistance training doesn't force the same physiological adaptation of muscle growth that can be seen in traditional strength training.

If we strength trained for three hours at a time, twice a day, five days per week for six months, we could expect to put on a lot of muscle mass. We would also gain some mass in the form of scar tissue as a result of straining muscles without adequate recovery. Average weight lifters tend to use very stable machines and load on as much weight as they can handle. Serious lifters work out as often as they can with the goal of putting on muscle mass.

However, if we resistance train functionally and intelligently for forty-five minutes to an hour at a time one to three days per week, we can effectively develop strength without affecting our overall mass. We might even lose some mass in the form of body fat. When we incorporate resistance training into our training program, we make muscle mass that we don't use on a regular basis more metabolically active.

The bottom line is that how we utilize resistance training and the time a muscle is placed under tension should be determined by our individual goals, needs, wants, and abilities. As we know, the demands of endurance sports are tremendous. We expose muscles, joints, and connective tissue to a great deal of stress, and we need to prepare our bodies beyond the demands of our sport. But we need to do so in a way that will allow us to utilize that strength in coordination with other muscles and stabilizers.

SPORT SPECIFICITY

It's clear that a high strength-to-weight ratio must be developed to achieve efficient muscle movement and reach our potential in endurance sports. An athlete who can lift 300 pounds and weighs 150 pounds is better off than an athlete who can lift 400 but weighs 250. You must be able to move your mass effectively to excel in most sports.

Functional resistance training is the most sport-specific way to strength train. Because we're training movements, we're forcing adaptations by our nervous system and integrating trunk and joint stabilizers. The end result will be that we can fully utilize our strength gains to enhance our performance. In other words, our nervous system can easily make the transition from the gym to our sport because we've developed strength in our primary movers in coordination with the joint and trunk stabilizers we use in our sport.

Developing strength functionally also allows us to maximize our time and energy in the gym. We can get a full-body workout in relatively little time because many exercises we perform involve multiple joints and muscles. When we integrate joint and trunk stabilizers, we recruit a lot of muscle mass at the same time, which in turn places a greater demand on our cardiovascular system. As a result, functional strength training not only makes more muscle mass metabolically active, and gets us in and out of the gym in less time, but can also train our anaerobic energy system.

STRENGTH DEVELOPMENT

Strength or resistance training is essential for both competitive and recreational athletes. It's important to develop full-body, overall strength to maintain symmetry and enhance performance. Before we can build strength, we need to create joint stability. Once we are strong and stable, we can develop sport-specific power.

TECHNIQUE

Every resistance training exercise should be performed with proper technique in mind. We never want to sacrifice our form in order to simply add more resistance or move on to a more complex movement than we're prepared to perform.

In general, all resistance training exercises should be performed in a slow and controlled manner. We want to avoid using parts of our body not associated with the motion. In other words, minimize the recruitment of supporting muscles, such as the trapezius muscles that will want to contract during many upper-body movements, so that you can maximize the demand placed on the targeted muscle. It's also important to control the eccentric or negative phase of any exercise. For instance, when we squat, we want to lower the weight slowly toward the floor before entering the concentric or positive phase of the movement. Also, as we discussed in previous chapters, we want to recruit the stabilizing musculature in our trunk and surrounding our joints during any exercise. Lastly, an important part of proper technique is to contract the muscle(s) you're attempting to target with any particular movement.

TEMPO, SETS, REPS, AND RESISTANCE

As mentioned earlier, time under tension affects the load placed on the muscle. *Tempo* is the speed at which a movement is performed. The tempo an exercise is performed at will be determined by the amount of resistance and the desired goal. For strength training, we can slow the tempo to overload the muscle, while power training requires a quick tempo to develop speed.

The sets and repetitions (reps) performed in a workout will also affect the load on the muscle. For example, two sets of fifteen reps at a medium weight and a slow tempo might be used to train muscle endurance. Three sets of eight reps at a heavy weight could be used to build muscle mass. For the most part, the number of sets and repetitions are less important than the tempo and resistance of the exercise.

Many times athletes will alternate muscle groups during a workout. This gives the muscle a chance to recover but still keeps the heart rate up and gets you out of the gym a little more quickly.

Overall, designing a program should be customized to a person's goals, needs, wants, and abilities. The sets, reps, tempo, and resistance are all factors that can change the intensity and intent of a workout. Just remember that the average endurance athlete doesn't want to train like the average guy in the weight room. Be selective in terms of what exercises you choose to do and how you choose to do them. Working out should be designed to enhance performance, not kill time.

VARIETY

Just as we recognize the importance of incorporating variety in other aspects of our crosstraining, we must continually challenge the nervous system in our strength training. This means varying the type of exercise, the angle at which it's performed, the amount of stability, the resistance, the number of sets and reps, as well as the tempo. As a result, the body is forced continually to adapt, which will help us maximize our gains and decrease monotony.

STRENGTH-TRAINING EXERCISES

As previously discussed, we must be sure not to let any increase in muscle strength decrease our flexibility or range of motion. Therefore, every resistance training session should start with at least five minutes of aerobic warmup and five to fifteen minutes of stretching. Each workout should end with a cooldown and a ten- to twenty-minute stretch. This practice will help prevent injuries while we're working out as well as keep us from becoming stiff-jointed muscleheads.

What follows are some examples of exercises that can help enhance endurance sport performance. Keep the resistance of each movement low when first starting out. It does us little good to increase the weight of an exercise at the expense of form and technique. Our goal is not only to make gains in strength but also to train the body in correct or sport-specific biomechanical positions. The last thing we want to do is create bad habits in the gym that could lead to injury or negatively impact our performance.

LOWER-BODY STRENGTH EXERCISES

7.1 | Single-Leg Leg Press with Disc: This exercise requires a leg press machine. Extend your legs upward from a seated position against resistance with a disc under one foot. Perform this exercise slowly, choose a weight that allows for a full range of motion, and make sure your knee is tracking over your second toe. Do not attempt a single-leg leg press until you have established proper technique with two legs.

7.1

7.2 | Single-Leg Cable Leg Curl: This exercise requires a cable machine. Place an ankle strap on one leg, facing away from the machine, and flex your leg while standing against resistance. Perform this exercise slowly. Choose a weight that allows for a full range of motion, and make sure your knee is tracking over your second toe.

7.3 | Single-Leg Fixed-Bar Squat: This exercise requires a squat machine that has a bar fixed to the squat cage that can slide up and down. Squat from a standing position against resistance. Perform this exercise slowly, choose a weight that allows for a full range of motion, and make sure your knee is tracking over your second toe and that your hips are level. Do not attempt a single-leg weighted squat until you have established proper technique with two legs.

7.4a

7.4 a,b | Eccentric Hamstrings:

This exercise requires a partner to hold your feet or a fixed, heavy object under which you can place your feet. Slowly lower yourself from a kneeling position toward the floor.

Maintain a neutral spine, make sure not to break at the waist, and keep your hands out in front of you. Once you've lowered yourself to the floor, push yourself back up to the starting position with your arms.

7.4b

7.5 | Dumbbell Matrix Lunges: Lunge at different angles while holding a dumbbell in each hand. Maintain a neutral spine, keep your chest up, and make sure your knee is tracking over your second toe. Alternate lunging forward, laterally, and diagonally to the rear. Weighted lunges should not be attempted until you have established proper technique performing lunges without weight.

UPPER-BODY STRENGTH EXERCISES

7.6

7.6 | Dumbbell Press While Bridging on Stability Ball: This exercise requires a stability ball and a pair of dumbbells. Lie faceup on the ball with your head and shoulders supported by the ball. Slowly press the weights from chest level until your arms are fully extended directly above your chest. Perform this exercise with very light weight at first until you have established proper technique. Always choose a weight that you can control and stabilize throughout a full range of motion.

7.7 | Standing Row: This exercise requires a cable machine. Pull the cable toward you from a half-squat position against resistance. Maintain a neutral spine, pull slowly, keep your spine stable and in the same place, relax your traps, keep your chest up, and squeeze your shoulder blades together at completion. Choose a weight that you can control and that allows you to perform a full range of motion.

7.7

7.8

7.8 | Single-Arm Cable Butterfly: This exercise requires a cable machine. Standing sideways to the machine, pull the cable inward with one arm against resistance. Maintain a neutral spine, relax your traps, and don't allow your upper body to rotate. Choose a weight that you can control and that allows you to perform a full range of motion.

7.9

7.9 | Single-Arm Cable Pull: This exercise requires a cable machine. Standing on one foot, pull the cable from high to low with your opposite arm against resistance. Maintain a neutral spine and level hips and shoulders, pull slowly, keep your spine stable and in the same place, relax your traps, keep your chest up, and squeeze your shoulder blades together at completion. Choose a weight that you can control and that allows you to perform a full range of motion.

7.10 | Single-Arm Cable Press: This exercise requires a cable machine. Standing in a split-stance position, press the cable out from waist level away from the machine. Maintain a neutral spine, keep your chest up, relax your traps, keep a slight bend in your knees, and keep your upper body stable and in the same position. Perform this exercise slowly, and choose a weight that you can control and that allows you to perform a full range of motion.

INSTABILITY

We can force our nervous system to recruit joint and trunk stabilizers when we strength train by adding an element of instability. We can incorporate instability into our strength training in numerous ways. One way is to perform an exercise by simply standing on one leg instead of two. Another way is to use a cable or dumbbell instead of a fixed bar or machine to perform a movement. We can also stand, kneel, or lie on an unstable surface such as a disc, foam roll, balance board, or stability ball.

Not every exercise in your workout needs to involve multiple joints and muscles to be beneficial. Also, not all exercises need to have an element of instability to be functional. However, as you progress, an easy way to continually challenge your nervous system is to make the same exercises and movements you already perform more unstable.

PERSONAL TRAINERS

There are some very knowledgeable, well-educated, focused, and passionate personal trainers out there. Unfortunately, they're the exception and not the rule. You need to be sure you know what you're getting with a trainer. He or she should be able to help you design a program based on your personal goals, not the trainer's predetermined programs. Then, a trainer should explain to you why the program was designed a certain way and how it will change as you progress. During each session you should be learning something new.

The best trainers are those who are committed to intelligently educating and empowering their clients. They have chosen to make the fitness profession a career because they enjoy helping people realize their health and wellness goals. Exceptional trainers usually have at least a four-year degree in kinesiology, physiology, or a similar subject and proactively seek out continuing education seminars. Educational background and experience are very important considerations when selecting a trainer. The title "certified personal trainer" often involves nothing more than passing a quiz.

Ideal trainers should take pride in their work and be constantly thinking of ways to maximize the time and energy you're spending with them. They should be 100 percent focused on their client 100 percent of the time. Great trainers are great listeners, mentally prepare for each client, and are always thinking ahead. They should be able to relate anything they do with you to your goals, needs, wants, and abilities. Ask your trainer questions periodically so that you're convinced he or she is maximizing your time and energy. Knowledgeable trainers won't be afraid to reveal that they don't know everything and will make an effort to find answers to your questions.

The very best trainers should spend the first one or two sessions doing a full-body physical assessment with you and should be constantly reassessing your movement patterns every time they see you. A personalized program and approach can only be accomplished once a trainer has analyzed your specific needs. At the very least, the trainer should analyze your gait by watching you walk and should spend ample time assessing your posture. A personal trainer's training program is only as effective as his or her assessment skills.

Trainers should be able to demonstrate everything they ask a client to do and should comment on form and the pace of reps. They should point out what you should be feeling in each muscle group as you're training so that you visualize what's happening as you stress each muscle. An effective cue is for a trainer to occasionally use his or her hands to touch the muscle to be targeted. When done in a professional and knowledgeable manner, this element of human touch can significantly improve your ability to contract a muscle. On the other hand, if you're uncomfortable with someone else touching you, say so and the trainer can just use more verbal cues.

A good trainer should be motivating you to get more out of every set and spotting you as required. He or she should be creative and have the ability to add variety to your program. If your trainer is just walking you over to your next set holding a clipboard, gazing off into the distance as you perform your sets, you have the wrong trainer.

A lot of trainers take the same approach with every client. They'll take some basic plan that they've learned from someone else and use it for a fifty-year-old sedentary person as well as an active twenty-five-year-old. Many trainers will simply train their clients like they train themselves or don't design a program that's specific for their client. Oftentimes, a trainer will emphasize his or her specialty as opposed to thinking critically about "movement" and individual goals.

Overall, don't be afraid to expect a lot from a personal trainer. As with any service, a good personal trainer should exceed your expectations and deliver value to you as a client.

SUPPLEMENTS

Supplementation inspires many differing views. One school of thought is that you can get everything you need for your body by eating the right foods. However, others believe that it's impossible to eat all the food necessary to get all of the nutrients you need.

What follows are brief discussions of some of the nutritional supplements most commonly used by endurance athletes. Before taking any supplement, do additional research, and make sure it makes sense and is safe for your use.

Protein

Protein is the single most important ingredient in new muscle development and as such plays an important role in our performance. Some endurance athletes will supplement the protein they ingest from food with protein powder shakes, bars, and other protein-fortified foods. Protein supplementation makes sense for those who find it difficult to get the amount of protein they need each day without ingesting excessive calories.

Protein intake is dependent on your activity level and the intensity of your workouts. As a general rule, endurance athletes should ingest approximately one-half to one gram of protein for each pound of body weight per day. Since our body doesn't store protein, we can't simply ignore ingesting protein one day and make it up the next.

Vitamins

Multivitamin and mineral supplements are very common and appear to be most beneficial to people who have difficulty eating a well-balanced diet. Overdosing on fat-soluble vitamins such as A, D, E, and K can be toxic and thus hazardous to your health, so you must be aware of the amount you are ingesting in the form of supplements, plus what you are obtaining from the food you eat. Water-soluble vitamins such as vitamin C can be taken in very large amounts and will likely only result in perhaps diarrhea or the production of fluorescent and expensive urine!

Antioxidants, such as vitamin C and vitamin E, are of tremendous importance in the body's defense against the muscle damage that occurs from exercise. Athletes who are doing intense training may benefit from the addition of antioxidant supplements to their diets.

Zinc and magnesium are two compounds that are also depleted through strenuous exercise. A zinc deficiency decreases muscle strength and endurance. Zinc promotes healing, tissue repair, and muscle growth. That burn you feel during exercise is lactic acid buildup in your muscles, and many of the enzymes that prevent the buildup of lactic acid require zinc.

A magnesium deficiency decreases oxygen delivery to muscle tissue. Magnesium promotes muscle strength and endurance and also activates enzymes necessary for the metabolism of carbohydrates and amino acids.

Other vitamins you should consider as supplements comprise the B complex group, used in the formation of every cell in your body: B1 (thiamine), B2 (riboflavin), B3 (niacin), B5 (pantothenic acid), B6 (pyridoxine), B7 (biotin), B12 (cobalamin), and folic acid (folate or folacin).

Creatine

Creatine phosphate, commonly known as simply creatine, is a high-energy phosphate compound that your body uses to rapidly resynthesize adenosine triphosphate (ATP), an immediate source of energy for muscle contraction. Creatine is an amino acid derivative found in the human body and in such foods as salmon, tuna, pork, and beef. Now available in many different forms, it has

TABLE 7.1

Daily Allowance for Vitamins and Minerals

U.S. Recommended Daily Allowances (RDAs) and the Suggested Optimal Daily Nutritional Allowances (SONAs)

NUTRIENT	MEN		WOMEN	
	RDA	SONA	RDA	SONA
FAT-SOLUBLE VITAMINS				
Vitamin A (RE, 1 RE = 1 microgram = 3.33 IU)	1,000	2,000	800	2,000
Beta-carotene (mg)	N/A	100	N/A	80
Vitamin D (microgram; 1 microgram = 40 IU)	5	24	5	24
Vitamin E (IU, 1 IU alpha tocopherol equivalent to 1 mg alpha tocopherol)	10	800	8	800
Vitamin K (mg)	80	80	65	65
WATER-SOLUBLE VITAMINS				
Vitamin C (mg)	60	800	60	1,000
Vitamin B12 (mg)	2	3	2	3
Folic acid (microgram)	200	2,000	180	2,000
Niacin (mg)	15	30	15	25
Pyridoxine (B6) (mg)	2	25	1.6	20
Riboflavin (B2) (mg)	1.4	2.5	1.2	2
Thiamin (B1) (mg)	1.2	9.2	1	9

table 7.1 continued

NUTRIENT	MEN		WOMEN	
	RDA	SONA	RDA	SONA
MINERALS				
Boron (mg)	N/A	2.5	N/A	3
Calcium (mg)	800	700	800	1,200
Chromium (microgram)	50-200	300	50-200	300
Copper (mg)	1.5-3.0	1.5-4.0	1.5-3.0	1.5-4.0
Iodine (microgram)	150	150	150	150
Iron (mg)	10	20	15	20
Magnesium (mg)	350	600	280	550
Manganese (mg)	2-5	10	2-5	10
Phosphorous (mg)	800	800	800	800
Potassium (mg)	99	200-500	99	200-500
Selenium (microgram)	70	250	55	200
Sodium (mg)	500	400	500	400
Zinc (mg)	15	20	12	17

NOTE: SONA WAS DEVELOPED BY ALEX SCHAUSS, PH.D., BASED ON A FIFTEEN-YEAR STUDY.

become an increasingly popular supplement among athletes. Some evidence indicates that it can help decrease the amount of recovery time needed after exercise. It has also been shown to cause cells to retain more fluid, giving the appearance of greater muscle mass. This fluid is usually lost within one to two weeks of discontinued use. There are conflicting studies and opinions as to whether it will enhance performance.

Caffeine

Caffeine is found in coffee, tea, cocoa, caffeinated sodas, and chocolate and has had a reputation for years as an effective performance enhancement supplement. Studies have shown that taken in the right amounts, caffeine increases adrenalin release, stimulates the central nervous system, and helps us utilize body fat as fuel, which aids in the conservation of glycogen. However, because caffeine is a diuretic, using it as a supplement should be done carefully.

According to some studies, caffeine in small doses may improve endurance by reducing glucose burning and increasing fat burning. One study, conducted on cyclists by Lars McNaughton in Australia, showed that ten milligrams of caffeine per kilogram of body weight taken three hours before exercise allowed the athletes to ride both longer and harder. However, research has also shown that if you already habitually use caffeine, then no amount of extra caffeine will benefit you. Yet other studies deny that it will aid performance for anyone.

Glucosamine and Chondroitin

Glucosamine is a building block used by the body to manufacture specialized molecules called *glycosaminoglycans*, found in cartilage. It's been used as a supplement by many injured athletes in a variety of sports. Some evidence suggests that it can help with the healing of ligament, tendon, cartilage, and muscle tears.

L-Glutamine

Glutamine is a nonessential amino acid, which means your body can create its own glutamine to a certain extent, on its own. It has been shown that after exercise glutamine levels fall off. This is important to note because glutamine is used to transport nitrogen to muscle tissues, which is important for protein synthesis as well as glycogen and oxygen uptake into muscle cells.

Nitric Oxide (NO_2)

Nitric oxide is a supplement designed to decrease recovery time between strenuous workouts. It supposedly facilitates protein synthesis by increasing oxygen and glycogen uptake into muscle cells.

L-Carnitine

L-carnitine is a substance made by the body that is used to transport fat. As a supplement, it has been used for years. Some research studies have concluded that it can enhance anaerobic and aerobic performance.

Ginseng

Ginseng, another popular supplement among endurance athletes, is an herb derived from three different plants. There are numerous types of ginseng, and many have been proven, among other things, to increase an athlete's use of body fat as an energy source. However, some sports nutritionists believe that ginseng will not benefit athletes whatsoever.

SAFETY

Resistance training workouts should be fun but also, more important, safe. Everything we do should have a purpose. Improper movement or loads can lead to acute and even chronic injuries. We need to progress the intensity of our workouts gradually in order for our body to be able to adapt to the stresses we place on it in our training. Poor exercise selection can lead to muscle imbalances, which will eventually result in musculoskeletal breakdowns and pain. Safe resistance training requires always being aware of the proper body positions and movements required in an exercise.

A functionally balanced training program will enhance our postural strength, coordination, balance, and performance. It will help us reduce musculotendinous, connective tissue, and neurological fatigue. Overall, be creative, have fun, and critically think of ways you can make your resistance training more effective and safe.

chapter 8
power

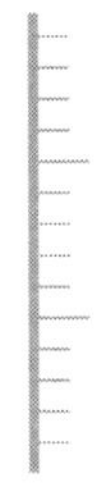

It never gets easier; you just go faster. —*Greg LeMond*

FAST- AND SLOW-TWITCH MUSCLE FIBERS

We all possess two types of muscle fiber, slow-twitch and fast-twitch. *Fast-twitch* fibers are activated during all-out exercise requiring rapid and powerful, anaerobic movements. In contrast, *slow-twitch* fibers are recruited to sustain continuous, aerobic activities. In most sports, we use both muscle fiber types. For example, we primarily utilize slow-twitch fibers when we maintain a steady pace and fast-twitch fibers when we start, accelerate up a hill, chase down a competitor, and sprint.

Why is this information important? Research has shown that through training we can alter the composition of our musculature to meet the demands of our particular sport. In other words, a sprinter can train to increase the percentage of fast-twitch muscle fibers in his legs, and a marathon runner can increase the percentage of slow-twitch in hers. Of course, there are genetic limitations to how much you can alter muscle composition, and there is a point at which certain performance elements will decrease. So, endurance sport athletes wouldn't want to spend a high percentage of their available training time developing their fast-twitch muscle fibers. However, if we completely ignore training these muscle fibers, they won't be very effective when we do call upon them. And, if we want to improve our ability to start, accelerate up a hill, chase down a competitor, or sprint, we need to train our muscles in such a way as to increase the amount of fast-twitch musculature at our disposal.

EXPLOSIVENESS

As we discussed in previous chapters, we first need to develop stability. Once we develop stability, we can develop strength. When we add the element of speed to our strength, we develop power or explosiveness. *Explosiveness* is the ability to exert maximal force as quickly as possible. In other words, strength plus speed equals power. It's possible to be strong and slow, or weak and quick, and not be powerful.

In endurance sports, we use our explosive power to start, accelerate, and sprint. In essence, we want to be as strong and as fast as we can for our body weight. It's all about power-to-weight ratio. The athlete who can move his or her mass the quickest, and produce the most force, will undoubtedly move the most powerfully.

It's important to have a high power-to-weight ratio versus just being powerful. For example, you might be able to throw a tire fifty feet. However, if you have a vertical jump of eight inches, you probably don't have the power-to-weight ratio necessary to win a field sprint.

SPEED DEVELOPMENT

As we know, developing speed and power is also dependent on technique. When we become more effective at performing our endurance sport movements at high speeds, we improve our overall efficiency. In other words, we need to improve our explosiveness, but we also need to train our nervous system to be able to recruit muscle fibers in sport-specific movements and more quickly than we actually use them in our sport. As we've discussed, we need to train beyond the demands of our sport to create adaptations that will enhance our performance.

Those of you who have ever played a musical instrument have more than likely experienced this concept firsthand. When you were first learning, you were slow and inefficient, because your nervous system was still learning the movement patterns necessary to play that instrument. However, with practice, you eventually became more efficient and could play a piece of music faster and faster. You eventually reached the point where you could play the piece much faster than required. And, when you played the piece at the pace it was supposed to be played, you were more accurate and efficient with your movements.

A runner who wants to improve his or her sprint needs to not only become more explosive but also needs to learn how to sprint. This involves proper use of the arms, running on the balls of your feet, and driving your knees. Arm movements are a vital component in sprinting. We swing our arms back and forth and bring them through the hips. They allow us to generate and maintain speed. When we stay on the balls of our feet, we're able to drive forward much more effectively. Lastly, sprinting involves driving our knees forward to full extension and then recovering quickly. It's this knee turnover that increases our revolutions per minute and results in faster running.

Cyclists need to learn proper technique for sprinting on a bike. If we're sloppy and inefficient when we sprint or throw the bike laterally more than necessary, we transfer less energy to the pedals. Swimmers need to learn how to increase their stroke rate without losing efficiency. Nordic skiers and in-line skaters need to be able to increase the frequency of their skate without getting sloppy.

ANAEROBIC ENERGY SYSTEM

So, what if you're content with your ability to start, accelerate, and sprint? That's excellent, but you can still use power training to further develop your much-needed anaerobic energy system. If you're like most endurance athletes, you spend the vast majority of your training time exercising your muscles aerobically or in the presence of oxygen. However, besides short bursts, there are times when we all go into oxygen debt. For instance, we're unable to meet the oxygen demands of working muscles when we climb a hill or kick to the finish.

We train this ability through interval training. Aerobic intervals help us increase our *anaerobic threshold*, or the point at which we switch to this anaerobic energy system. Anaerobic intervals also help us improve our *lactate threshold*, or the ability of our muscles to contract in a more acidic environment.

Power training not only teaches our nervous system to recruit muscle quickly but also stresses our anaerobic energy system maximally. When we train our explosiveness, we place a tremendous load on the body neurologically and physiologically that results in more efficient energy system pathways at lower intensity levels. For example, during a lower-body power workout, we open a huge amount of the capillaries in our quads and glutes. Eventually, this type of training results in cardiovascular adaptations being made as our body attempts to deliver more blood, more quickly, to meet the demands being placed on these muscles. Now, when we recruit the same muscles during a hard effort less intensely, we're able to stay aerobic longer. Since our muscles are accustomed to maximal loads, they will be able to contract efficiently in a more acidic environment than before.

REACTIVE NEUROMUSCULAR TRAINING

Another term for power training is *reactive neuromuscular training*. This can be defined as a quick, powerful movement involving an eccentric contraction followed immediately by an explosive concentric contraction. Reactive neuromuscular training improves the reactivity of the neuromuscular system, enhances the rate of force production, and increases muscular function.

As with other forms of crosstraining, power training is often ignored by endurance athletes. Many are afraid that power training will result in muscle weight gain, lack of flexibility, and injury. These are misconceptions that have been developed from watching power lifting and strongman competitions.

Reactive neuromuscular training for endurance athletes involves being able to utilize the muscle we already possess more quickly and efficiently, not adding more muscle mass. Flexibility need not be affected by any type of crosstraining provided that you train muscles in full ranges of motion and be sure to warm up, cool down, and stretch. Lastly, power training can help you prevent injury as it will improve overall athleticism, function, and movement.

SPORT SPECIFICITY

As we discussed earlier, we want to train with our sport in mind. This means that we need to look at the forces involved in our sport to determine how we can best prepare for those demands. For example, both swimming and football require athletes to be powerful. However, since swimming isn't a contact sport, and because swimmers need to develop and maintain a much higher level of endurance and aerobic capacity, they'll want to spend a much smaller percentage of their total training time and take a much different approach to developing explosiveness.

In any physical activity, athletes should analyze the cost and benefit of what they do. In other words, what will we gain from training a particular way, and what are the potential risks? For instance, I don't recommend that endurance athletes learn Olympic-type power lifts with heavy weight. Although these movements can be great for athletes in some sports, I find the cost of performing such a lift with imperfect technique outweighs the benefit to those of us in endurance sports.

POWER DEVELOPMENT

Developing explosive power is essential for both the competitive and recreational endurance athlete. However, before we can develop power, we need to have a solid strength base in order to prevent injury and maximize explosiveness. Respect the progression, and resist the urge to jump ahead. Safe and effective power training requires strong and stable joints. Improving power requires adaptations by our muscle, connective tissue, nervous system, and energy systems. As a result, they all need to be prepared gradually for explosive movements. The first step is to build an adequate aerobic, agility, anaerobic, flexibility, joint stability, strength, and trunk stability base. We can then progress from the most basic power exercises to those that are higher impact.

TEMPO, SETS, REPS, AND RESISTANCE

As with strength training, the way we train to improve power is vital. The tempo should always be quick since we're attempting to marry strength and speed. The sets and reps should be low to ensure that each effort is at maximal intensity and to prevent overuse injuries. The resistance used in your workouts should be relatively light. We don't want to sacrifice speed for the sake of loading up the weight. In fact, your body weight can be more than sufficient resistance for a multitude of power exercises.

POWER TRAINING EXERCISES

The best way to improve our explosive power is through plyometric training. *Plyometrics* entails quick, powerful movements involving an eccentric contraction followed immediately by an explosive concentric contraction. Jumping is an example of lower-body plyometrics. When you jump, you take off and land. The takeoff involves a concentric contraction of your muscles to accelerate your body weight. Upon landing, your muscles contract eccentrically to help you decelerate. Through training, we can shorten the time between the two contractions to become more explosive. Throwing and catching a medicine ball with someone, or against a wall or trampoline, are examples of upper-body plyometrics.

Numerous plyometric exercises are ideal for developing power. As with any aspect of your training, I urge you to think critically, be creative, stay safe, think sport-specifically, and above all, have fun!

Guidelines for Plyometric Training

- *Drills affecting a particular muscle or joint should not be performed two days in a row.*
- *Allow time for complete recovery between sets.*
- *Use footwear and landing surfaces with good shock absorption.*
- *Warm up thoroughly before performing any plyometric exercises.*
- *Proper technique is essential and should never be sacrificed.*
- *Develop speed and control before increasing resistance and complexity.*
- *The time spent in contact with the floor or medicine ball should be as short as possible.*
- *The time spent in contact with the floor or medicine ball should be as quiet as possible.*
- *Make sure your spine and pelvis are stabilized by your trunk musculature at all times.*
- *Be aware of posture and body positions during all drills.*

LOWER-BODY POWER EXERCISES

8.1b

8.1a

8.1 a, b | Jump Rope Four-Square: Place two lines of tape on the floor perpendicular to one another. Jump rope from square to square in all directions; jump laterally, fore and aft, and diagonally. Maintain a neutral spine, and stay light on your feet.

Double-Leg Stair Hops: Hop up stairs with both legs; land soft and controlled with a neutral spine and with your knees tracking over your second toe. To increase difficulty, skip multiple stairs or hold onto a medicine ball.

Single-Leg Stair Hops: Hop up stairs with one leg at a time; land soft and controlled with a neutral spine and with your knee tracking over your second toe. To increase difficulty, skip multiple stairs or hold onto a medicine ball.

8.2 | Vertical Jumps: Jump up onto a stable box or bench; land soft and controlled with a neutral spine and with your knees tracking over your second toe. To increase difficulty, jump onto a higher box or hold onto a medicine ball.

8.3 | Lateral Jumps over a Bench: Jump laterally over a bench; land soft and controlled with a neutral spine and with your knees tracking over your second toe. To increase difficulty, jump over a higher bench or hurdle or hold onto a medicine ball.

8.2

8.3

UPPER-BODY POWER EXERCISES

8.4

Single-Arm Medicine Ball Throws with a Partner or Trampoline: Alternate throwing a light medicine ball with one arm overhead to a partner or against a trampoline. Relax your traps and decelerate the ball slowly. To increase difficulty, throw a heavier ball.

8.4 | Explosive Medicine Ball Bench Push-ups with a Partner: Kneel in front of a bench with your knees far enough away from the bench that you can perform a push-up with a neutral spine and without breaking at your waist. After each explosive push-up, have your partner throw the ball to you at chest level, catch the ball, and throw it back to your partner as quickly as possible before your next push-up. Minimize the time your hands are on the bench and that the medicine ball is in your hands.

8.5 a, b | Clapping Push-ups: Perform an explosive push-up on a soft surface. Push your chest far enough from the floor to allow you to clap before landing again; land soft and controlled, and explode off the floor again immediately. Maintain a neutral spine. To decrease difficulty, perform this exercise on your knees without breaking at your waist.

8.5a

8.5b

8.6 | Explosive 45-degree Pull-up: This exercise requires a fixed bar at roughly waist level. Hold onto the bar at chest level with a neutral spine and without breaking at your waist. Hang down with your arms extended, and explosively pull your chest up to the bar. Once your chest is at the top, grab the bar and slowly descend to the starting position. To decrease difficulty, raise the bar; to increase difficulty, lower the bar or raise your legs.

Explosive Fixed Bar Incline Press: This exercise requires a machine with a fixed bar that can slide up and down on a track. Sit faceup on an incline bench so that the bar is at chest level above you. Perform an explosive incline press, allowing the bar to float up its track. Catch the bar and control the weight's descent back to the starting position. Have someone spot you to prevent the bar from rotating and letting the hooks that adjust the bar's level catch back on the machine. Maintain a neutral spine, and choose a weight that you can control.

POWER AND HYDRATION

As endurance athletes, we know how important it is to stay hydrated. Our bodies consist of 60 to 70 percent water, and 70 to 75 percent of our muscle tissue is composed of water. As a result, it's no wonder that water is essential not only to control our core temperature but also to maintain proper muscle function, force production, efficiency, and power.

Most people are constantly a little dehydrated. We need to keep an ideal amount of fluid in our bodies to maximize physical performance and facilitate a multitude of basic physiological processes.

Water volume in our blood plays an important role in transporting oxygen and nutrients to our muscles. When we're dehydrated, our blood volume is lower. If we exercise when we're dehydrated, it's common to feel sluggish since our muscles aren't getting enough oxygen and nutrients to function at a faster pace. Additionally, waste products that are created when our muscles contract aren't being flushed from the muscle effectively. Research has proven that even slight dehydration can cause decreased physical performance. This is because a dehydrated muscle loses contractile strength, and less water in the body equates to lower blood volume. Losing contractile strength can obviously result in weakness. Lower blood volume means that the body will have a more difficult time getting oxygen to working muscles, which will undoubtedly affect speed, power, strength, and endurance.

Studies have found that to maintain a healthy hydration level, we need to drink eight to ten eight-ounce glasses of water per day and an additional twelve ounces for every half hour of exercise. However, other factors require us to drink more than these recommendations.

Exercising hard on a warm day, when the air is dry, can quickly lead to a significant loss of water in the system. Fluid is lost through the skin in the form of sweat as well as during respiration. Sweating is our body's way of cooling itself. The amount of perspiration depends on how strenuous the activity is, air temperature, air humidity, body composition, physiology, genetics, and whether we are accustomed to exercise. Contrary to popular belief, studies have shown that avid exercisers tend to sweat more quickly and profusely than sedentary adults. This is because the body is very intent on maintaining a constant core temperature and will eventually adapt to the stress of physical activity. In other words, the more active you are, the more sensitive your "cooling system."

We also lose water from our body when we breathe. With every exhalation, moisture is lost to the atmosphere. When the air is dry, this water is not replaced by the next inhalation. Even if you weren't exercising and were just sitting on the porch, you could become significantly dehydrated within a few hours simply by breathing.

We also lose vital minerals and electrolytes such as salt through our perspiration. As a result, many endurance athletes use an energy replacement drink to hydrate rather than just water before, during, and after strenuous workouts. Numerous such products are on the market. Avoid sports drinks that contain high levels of simple sugars like glucose or sucrose because they inhibit absorption of water by your body. The gas in carbonated drinks like soda also slows down absorption. Fructose/glucose polymer drinks work best because they contain fewer carbohydrates and small amounts of certain minerals and electrolytes that have been shown to enhance fluid absorption.

A simple way to help replenish what is lost through perspiration during the day is to drink diluted fruit juice. At first, the taste may not appeal to you, but after a while most people grow to prefer drinking juice diluted by at least 50 percent. In general, juice is bottled in concentrations too high for your body to maximally absorb the water in it as well as the various vitamins and minerals.

Diuretics are substances that draw water from your system. The most commonly ingested diuretics are alcohol and caffeine. Drinking diuretics can lead to dehydration. One of the most common dehydration scenarios is drinking alcohol the night before and then downing some coffee the next morning to fire the system up before a training session. When you drink little or no water in combination with this routine, you're sure to become very dehydrated.

Many endurance athletes will start hydrating a few hours before a hard training session or competitive event. A good rule of thumb is to drink an eight-ounce glass of water every fifteen minutes starting four hours before the workout and stopping twenty minutes before strenuous exercise.

In the name of comfort, you'll want to avoid having a full bladder during your workout. Be sure to sip rather than gulp to avoid swallowing a lot of air, which can disturb stomach function and slow absorption.

Staying well hydrated will help maximize physical performance as well as aid in basic physiological functions. Most people wouldn't think of driving around with too little coolant in their car's radiator but often never think twice about keeping their own system hydrated.

VARIETY

Because power training involves adaptations by the nervous system as well as muscles and connective tissue, it's imperative that we make an effort to vary our exercises. Once our nervous system adjusts to the physical demands we place on it, we need to add more stress and complexity to our exercises to achieve the most benefit. Variety keeps us challenged and will eventually yield the greatest results. If we continually raise the bar in all aspects of our crosstraining, we can expand our comfort zone and in turn enhance our performance.

chapter 9 mental training

All that a man achieves and all that he fails to achieve is the direct result of his own thoughts. —James Allen

PERFORMANCE ENHANCEMENT

Thus far, we have discussed physical preparation in depth. In recent years, endurance sports have increased in popularity both recreationally and competitively. Marketing and sponsorship have brought money to our sports, which has in turn motivated athletes to seek a competitive edge. Typical endurance athletes are independent, motivated, and excel at seeking ways to push themselves farther physically. However, to truly reach our performance potential, we also need to develop our psychological skills.

How many accomplished endurance athletes step up to the starting line doubting whether their preparation was adequate? How many competitors are intimidated by the confidence of others?

We all need to determine what state of mind allows us to train and race to our potential. Both competitive and recreational athletes can benefit from building more confidence in their abilities. For example, most elite-level endurance athletes find it necessary to avoid distractions, such as wonder what their competitors are doing, and focus on their own training and racing strategies in order to perform optimally.

Regardless of our goals, each of us needs to develop our own mental game plan. The essentials of such a plan involve learning ways to relax, concentrate, and image more effectively.

RELAXATION

Relaxation strategies are incredibly important for endurance athletes to develop as part of their mental game plan. We all experience some level of emotional and psychological stress due to family, work, and other life-related pressures. It's also very common to feel anxious before competition or a particularly difficult training session. Recreational and competitive athletes who are driven also develop performance expectations and have a strong desire to perform at that level. Often we're unable to control these thoughts and feelings, and we can become overly stressed. The muscular tension and cardiovascular response that result from such anxiety can adversely affect all aspects of our performance.

One example of a relaxation strategy is rhythmic breathing. This exercise can easily be done before and perhaps even during a workout or race. Breathing exercises have proven to be very effective in reducing anxiety. For instance, when tension is noticed, take three to five very deep or diaphragmatic breaths. Inhale to a count of four, hold for a count of four, exhale for a count of four, and pause for a count of four before repeating the sequence. When we control our breathing, we're able to release a lot of the muscle tension we've developed and bring our heart rate back down to normal.

CONCENTRATION

Concentration strategies are also crucial for us to develop. When we're focused, our analytical skills, technique, efficiency, and overall performance all improve.

However, we all have to learn how to prevent internal and external distracters from affecting our focus and concentration. External distracters such as other competitors, the weather, spectators, race officials, vehicles, and announcement speakers can all affect our ability to concentrate. Many of us also struggle with internal distracters such as negative self-talk or pessimistic thought processes. Whether internal or external, these distracters can result in our being unable to focus on what we need to perform our best.

We will perform our best when we stay focused on elements within our control. There are factors outside our control that can obviously influence our performance. However, if we spend too much time and energy concentrating on such things, we run the risk of neglecting the factors we can control. This in turn results in us diluting our focus, and ultimately our performance suffers.

One example of a concentration strategy we can utilize is *attentional cuing,* before or during a training session or race. Verbal or kinesthetic, attentional cues are used to retrigger focus once it has been lost. These cues can help us center our attention on the most appropriate aspects of the task at hand. For instance, we might find it beneficial to concentrate on a particular aspect of our technique during a particularly difficult effort. Perhaps our attentional cue would be a word or phrase that aids us in focusing on certain key elements that are most critical to performing optimally. For example, a triathlete might use an attentional cue of "heel strike" to help her get into a running rhythm after just getting off the bike portion of their event. Or, any endurance athlete might use the act of slapping his quads before the start of an event as an attentional cue to help focus on getting a strong start.

POSITIVE SELF-TALK

Self-talk is what we tell ourselves or think about before, during, and after an event. We can enhance performance by using positive self-talk to develop more confidence, for instance. Identifying areas where we need more confidence and then creating some related, positive statements to say or write on a regular basis can develop good self-talk. It's essential that any affirmation be stated strongly and in the present tense.

Athletes in countless sports have realized the benefits of replacing negative thoughts with positive ones. It does us no good to think about what we don't want to happen or things that are out of our control. In a way, our brain is like a computer. The better the data or instructions, the sweeter the results!

Positive Statements

I love racing in the rain.

I have an advantage on a course like this.

I perform my best under pressure.

IMAGERY

The use of mental rehearsal strategies can also be very effective for endurance athletes. For instance, all athletes could benefit from rehearsing the course of a race and how they will perform overall in an event in their mind. When we rehearse such things, we prepare not only our mind but also to some extent our body for what we will experience. In other words, if we can simulate what a race will look and feel like and how we will respond physically and mentally, we will be better prepared to meet the demands of the event.

An example of a mental rehearsal strategy that we can employ is visualization. *Visualization* consists of imagining all of the elements of a successful performance in great detail. Such imagery could take place any time before a training session or competition. We want to use as many senses as possible in creating the event in our mind. For example, a triathlete who's visualized extensively might be able to actually smell the sea air and taste the saltwater of an ocean swim during an imagery session.

It's also very important to visualize ourselves achieving certain performance goals we've set for an event. For instance, if we've been working on an element of our technique in training, we need to visualize ourselves effectively executing that technical element in the race.

PRECOMPETITION ROUTINE

Race day can be stressful for many athletes. Besides the anxiety of wanting to do well, you're concerned with making sure you have everything and are in the right place at the right time and umpteen other things. A good way to manage the stress and help you stay organized is to develop a precompetition routine. This can be likened to when a jet is on autopilot mode. A routine will allow you to relax more and simplify, which will in turn help you focus on what's important.

Through experience, you'll be able to create a system for the most optimal way to prepare for an event. For example, you might want to warm up and stretch a certain number of minutes before the start. Perhaps you'll get into a habit of getting away from everyone at some point so that you can relax, concentrate, and visualize what you're trying to accomplish. A lot of athletes also use music to get psyched up or calm nerves before competition.

Your precompetition routine might seem somewhat generic and forced at first, but in time you'll be able to customize and tweak it so that it becomes more comfortable. You may even decide that you perform best when there's little or no structure to what you do the day before and the day of an event. Whatever your race day preparation includes, it should put you in a frame of mind that will lead to total domination!

GOAL SETTING

The goals we set for ourselves have a lot to do with our mental outlook. *Short-term* goals are goals we want to achieve in the near future. *Long-term* goals are those that we set for several weeks, months, or even years from now. It's important to set both types of goals. Long-term goals help us stay on track, and short-term goals give us a way to measure our progress.

It's also imperative that we set *performance* goals as opposed to only outcome goals. Outcome goals, the most common goals that athletes set, can be a great way of keeping us motivated leading up to an event. However, since numerous factors are outside our control when it comes to how we will place, outcome goals can also make us feel as if we didn't perform well when we did. In other words, we may have had the race of our lives, but because we can't control how others perform, we might not finish in the top ten, do better than last year, or beat Joe.

Outcome Goals

To finish in the top ten

To do better than I did last year

To beat Joe Shmo

Performance goals are based on factors that are within our control. This type of goal setting will empower us a lot more and is a better measure of our success. The bottom line is that when we set and achieve realistic performance goals, our outcome goals become more attainable.

Performance Goals

To pace myself better than I did in my last race

To race as well as I've been training

To finish every race feeling as if I had nothing left to give

Filling out a form such as the goal summary here and referring to it occasionally can be a great tool for keeping us on track.

Goal Summary

date / /

What is your long-term dream goal in the sport?

What is your dream goal for this season?

What is a realistic goal that you can achieve this season?

What are three aspects of your physical performance that you would like to improve this season?

Set a goal that you can achieve in training within the next month.

Set a goal that you would like to accomplish in each training session.

How many competitive events would you like to enter this season?

Which events are the most important to you?

What is an important psychological goal for you to focus on this season in training?

What is an important psychological goal for you to focus on this season in competition?

TRAINING LOGS

Athletes in most sports keep a log of the factors that can affect their performance. This is a great way to see patterns in your training or races so that you can design a better program in the future. For example, if you notice that you usually aren't performing well when the bigger events come along, perhaps you can tweak your training to prevent that from happening in the future.

A good training log should allow you to keep track of any physical and psychological factors that you think might affect your performance. However, it also needs to be fairly easy to read and not too time-consuming to fill out. In Appendix A you will find an example of a training log that I developed for some of the athletes I've coached.

The left column has areas to keep track of your pulse in the morning to see how your body is responding to training. Your resting pulse should be taken before you get out of bed each morning. Your standing pulse should be taken as soon as you stand up from your bed. Both pulse rates need only be taken for fifteen seconds.

If you make a habit of doing this measurement every day and are consistent in how you take these two pulse rates, you can begin to see a pattern. For example, when you're rested, you might see resting pulses of between twelve and fourteen and standing pulses of between fifteen and seventeen. However, you might find that when you're training hard, your resting pulse will only climb slightly, but your standing pulse will shoot up significantly. When we're well rested, our heart won't react much to the added load of having to pump blood against gravity. However, when we're becoming fatigued, our heart will tend to overreact when we stand up.

For many athletes, pulse rates can be a great objective indicator of how their body's handling training stress. It's a great way to see if your body's becoming fatigued before you actually feel tired.

The left column of the training log also has areas to keep track of how many hours you sleep and your weight. The second column has spaces to keep track of what you eat during the day. Many athletes find it useful to track such things because these factors can significantly affect their performance.

The third column is where you can note that day's workout, and the fourth column cites how many hours were planned and accomplished. This column also has a box that allows you to give the workouts a subjective rating. Finally, the last column is a comments area where you can write down other thoughts or feelings that you might want to look back on in the future.

The last section of the training log gives you a chance to summarize the week overall. This is a great way to take inventory of the big picture every week. As a general rule, you want to take the time to analyze your training log at the end of every block of training to see if you can see patterns developing. At the end of the year, you can then determine what was done well and what elements of your training need to improve for the following year.

MENTAL CROSSTRAINING

Just as we discussed the need for physical crosstraining, it's also important to crosstrain mentally. For example, a sport like golf can help us improve our ability to relax, concentrate, or visualize. Applying mental training strategies in a variety of situations will increase your awareness and understanding of the techniques while improving your ability to utilize them.

END RESULT

As endurance sports increase in popularity, a growing number of us will focus on the mental aspects of our performance. It is clear that having a mental game plan can aid in achieving one's potential. Relaxation, concentration, and imagery strategies can be extremely useful mental training tools. When combined with effective physical preparation, psychological preparation can mean the difference between disappointment and attaining your goals.

chapter 10

designing a crosstraining program

Have a dream. Make a plan. Go for it. You'll get there, I promise.

–Zoe Koplowitz (a woman with multiple sclerosis who finished the 1993 New York City Marathon on crutches)

GOALS, NEEDS, WANTS, AND ABILITIES

We know that to maximize our time and energy, we need to design an effective training program. Any athlete who trains aimlessly will find it very difficult to ever reach his or her potential.

Ultimately, any training program you follow should be based on your individual goals, needs, wants, and abilities. The effectiveness of your training program will be limited by your analysis of these four factors. It sounds like common sense, right? However, many endurance athletes don't take the time to identify what their individual goals, needs, wants, and abilities are and how these factors will affect how they train.

To identify our goals, needs, wants, and abilities, we need to think critically and be honest with ourselves. We need to look at the big picture and ask some tough questions: What are our short- and long-term goals? Are our goals performance related or only outcome driven? What aspects of our performance do we need to emphasize? Have we identified and taken our limiting factors into account? Do we want our training to be varied and fun? Have we prioritized our wants? How many hours per week are we able to train? How much training are we physically able to handle in one day, week, or month? The answers to such questions become the foundation for building a customized and effective training program.

Let's say one of our goals is to improve our posture because we know it will help us decrease our risk for injury and increase our efficiency and force production. Let's assume, too, that we don't have any gross flexibility and strength imbalances that are affecting our posture but that we recognize the need to develop more strength and stability in our trunk musculature. We want to work on our core at home on our recovery days, Monday and Friday. We also want to do trunk workouts on Wednesday and Sunday, the two days we go to the gym. Now, let's say we've looked at all of our other time commitments and determined that we're able to spend one hour of our total training time per week to accomplishing this goal. One of our options would then be to design four fifteen-minute trunk strength and stability workouts to do per week. Two of the workouts would be composed of exercises that we could do at home, and the other two would take advantage of the equipment in the gym.

LIMITING FACTORS

We all have strengths and weaknesses. When our weaknesses have a negative impact on our performance, we refer to them as *limiting factors*. It's essential that we identify what these limiting factors are and address them in our training program.

For instance, let's say a triathlete finds herself consistently finishing around the middle of the field in every race. She's usually one of the first out of the water but ends up starting the run near the tail end of the field. She quickly realizes that if she can avoid getting passed on the bike, she'll be much more competitive. However, simply recognizing that she's a weak cyclist isn't very useful. This athlete also needs to be able to identify specifically what needs to be improved. Once she does that, she must commit to strengthening this limiting factor by developing a training program that will address it effectively.

Many athletes spend way too much time training their strengths and very little time on anything else. This is why a lot of athletes tend to reach performance plateaus. Improving our limiting factors isn't a lot of fun because it involves spending time training aspects of performance in which we don't excel. It can be difficult, painful, time-consuming, and frustrating. However, it's essential if we want to continue to progress as an athlete.

TRAINING PROGRAM EVALUATION

Before we begin designing our crosstraining program, we want to evaluate the various factors that we need to take into consideration. If we dive into constructing the specifics of our program without critically thinking about the bigger picture, we're bound to create an ineffective and unrealistic training plan. Filling out a form such as the one here can give us a starting point from which to develop the parameters of our program. Once we've identified the variables that will affect our plan, we can refer back to this information as we design the specifics of our program.

PROGRAM DESIGN

Worthwhile training programs are designed and customized with your goals, needs, wants, and abilities in mind. There are no quick fixes, but an individualized training program, combined with hard work, dedication, and motivation, will make a world of difference!

Designing a training program can get complicated. We need to decide what training element we want to work on each day and then how to design each workout. See the guidelines on designing a training program on pages 144–45.

Training Program Evaluation Form

Background and experience in your sport:

Short-term goals

Long-term goals

Physical strengths

Physical limiting factors

How much time do you have each day to train in your sport?

Mon.	Tues.	Wed.	Thur.	Fri.	Sat.	Sun.

How much time do you have each day to crosstrain?

Mon.	Tues.	Wed.	Thur.	Fri.	Sat.	Sun.

Intensity and duration of crosstraining activities you enjoy on a regular basis

______

______

______

Rate the following from 1 to 5
(1/poor; 2/fair; 3/average; 4/very good; 5/excellent)

Aerobic ______ Anaerobic ______ Flexibility ______ Balance ______

Agility ______ Trunk strength ______ Upper-body strength ______

Lower-body strength ______ Power ______

Past/current injuries to consider

______

______

______

Guidelines for Designing a Training Program

- ***Our muscles and cardiovascular system need time*** to recover. Our body makes the greatest adaptations and gains during periods of rest that follow strenuous training. If we continue to overload the system without taking the time to recover, we will quickly plateau. The amount of recovery between resistance training workouts depends on the volume and intensity of your workout. As a general rule, strenuous workouts such as sprints, intervals, resistance training, and power training shouldn't be performed two days in a row. Pushing the limits of and fatiguing the same muscle group two days in a row results in muscle breakdown and doesn't give it an opportunity to rebuild.

- ***Just as we design the specifics of our endurance***, interval, and sprint workouts to achieve the best results, we need to put some thought into how we design our crosstraining workouts. In most cases, we want to perform integrated exercises, or movements that involve using many muscles at the same time, earlier in our workout. An exercise such as a squat requires the recruitment of secondary and stabilizing muscles as well as the neuromuscular system. The latter part of your workout should be reserved for exercises that attempt to emphasize a particular muscle, such as a bicep curl. This ensures that we don't prefatigue muscles that are needed in those integrated movement patterns.

- ***Once you're unable to perform an exercise*** with perfect technique, you're done. Don't think of it as a failure; on the contrary, think of it as a success because you've obviously accomplished the goal of fatiguing the targeted muscle(s).

- ***Your program should build in terms of volume and intensity*** for three weeks, and then you should give yourself a "relative" recovery week. This recovery week is where all the adaptations in response to the hard work you've done will take place.

- ***If you want to maximize your time and energy*** during crosstraining workouts, your heart should be pumping throughout your workout. This is best accomplished by forcing the body to recruit stabilizing musculature or by combining two exercises. For example, instead of just doing a lunge, grab some dumbbells and do a biceps curl while you lunge. Or instead of using a bench, use a stability ball when performing a dumbbell bench press.

- ***You don't necessarily need a gym full of equipment*** to get a good workout. If you're on the road or don't have time to drive to the gym, you can improvise. Your body weight and some dumbbells can provide plenty of resistance to give you a challenging workout if you use a little creativity.

- ***Train your weaknesses as well as your strengths.*** Almost everyone regardless of their sport needs some degree of aerobic, agility, anaerobic, balance, body awareness, coordination, endurance, flexibility, functional, nervous system, posture, power, strength, and trunk stability training.
- ***Incorporate some instability into your workouts*** with foam rolls, stability balls, and medicine balls so that you keep your nervous system on its toes.
- ***Everything you do should have a purpose.*** For example, a resistance training program that consists solely of multiple repetitions with fixed machines can be great for isolated muscle development. However, keep in mind that this isn't always the most effective way to reach your goals.
- ***Address faulty body positions and movements.*** Select exercises that will help you correct muscle imbalances and asymmetries that will eventually result in pain. Improper movements or loads can cause acute and chronic injuries.
- ***Keep your program fun, safe, and varied.*** This approach will help you stay motivated and will produce the best results.

PERIODIZATION

Periodization involves designing a training program in which the volume and intensity of workouts on certain days or during particular weeks are cycled. For example, a four-week block of training will generally become gradually more difficult from the first to third week and then relatively easy the fourth week. The third week of the program is the most challenging and may involve a training overload. The fourth week is essentially a recovery week. This recovery time is necessary to allow the body to make adaptations to the hard work it's done. Many athletes who don't periodize their training become flat or sluggish and are at a greater risk of overtraining.

Periodizing Training throughout the Week (Microcycle)

Monday	Active rest or complete recovery
Tuesday	Low volume, high intensity
Wednesday	High volume, low intensity
Thursday	Medium volume, medium intensity
Friday	Active rest or complete recovery
Saturday	Low volume, high intensity
Sunday	High volume, low intensity

Periodizing a Four-Week Block of Training (Macrocycle)

Week 1	Medium volume, medium intensity
Week 2	Medium/high volume, medium/high intensity
Week 3	High volume, high intensity
Week 4	Low volume, low intensity

Periodizing Macrocycles throughout the Year

3 macrocycles	Conditioning phase	Medium volume, medium intensity
4 macrocycles	Preparation phase	High volume, medium intensity
1 macrocycle	Specialization phase	Medium volume, high intensity
4 macrocycles	Competition phase	Medium volume, high intensity
1 macrocycle	Recovery phase	Very low volume and intensity

Periodizing Four Years of Training, with Year 4 as Most Important

Year 1	Medium volume, medium intensity
Year 2	Higher volume, higher intensity
Year 3	Highest volume, highest intensity
Year 4	Less volume, less intensity

Example of a conditioning phase macrocycle of training for a competitive endurance athlete:

TABLE 10.1 **Microcycle 1** | Conditioning Phase

DAY	ACTIVITY	TIME	INTENSITY	INTENT
MON	Visualization	30 minutes	Low	Mental Training
	Stretch	15 minutes	Low	Flexibility
TUES	Soccer	1.0 hour	High	Aerobic/Anaerobic
	Power Workout	30 minutes	High	Power
	Strength Workout	30 minutes	Medium	Strength
	Core Workout	10 minutes	Medium	Trunk Stabilization
	Stretch	15 minutes	Low	Flexibility
WED	Endurance Workout	2.0 hours	Medium	Endurance
	Stability Workout	30 minutes	Medium	Joint Stabilization
	Stretch	10 minutes	Low	Flexibility
THURS	Tempo Workout	1.5 hours	Medium	Aerobic Capacity
	Core Workout	10 minutes	Medium	Trunk Stabilization
	Stretch	10 minutes	Low	Flexibility
FRI	Easy Aerobic	30 minutes	Low	Recovery
	Agility Workout	30 minutes	Medium	Agility
	Stretch	15 minutes	Low	Flexibility
SAT	Aerobic Intervals	1.5 hours	Medium	Anaerobic Threshold
	Strength Workout	1.0 hour	Medium	Strength
	Core Strength	10 minutes	Medium	Trunk Stabilization
	Stretch	15 minutes	Low	Flexibility
SUN	Endurance Workout	2.5 hours	Medium	Endurance
	Balance Workout	30 minutes	Low	Balance
	Stretch	10 minutes	Low	Flexibility

TABLE 10.2 Microcycle 2 | Conditioning Phase

DAY	ACTIVITY	TIME	INTENSITY	INTENT
MON	Visualization	30 minutes	Low	Mental Training
	Stretch	15 minutes	Low	Flexibility
TUES	Soccer	1.0 hour	High	Aerobic/Anaerobic
	Power Workout	30 minutes	High	Power
	Strength Workout	30 minutes	Medium	Strength
	Core Workout	10 minutes	Medium	Trunk Stabilization
	Stretch	15 minutes	Low	Flexibility
WED	Endurance Workout	2.5 hours	Medium	Endurance
	Stability Workout	30 minutes	Medium	Joint Stabilization
	Stretch	10 minutes	Low	Flexibility
THURS	Tempo Workout	2.0 hours	Medium	Aerobic Capacity
	Core Workout	10 minutes	Medium	Trunk Stabilization
	Stretch	10 minutes	Low	Flexibility
FRI	Easy Aerobic	30 minutes	Low	Recovery
	Agility Workout	30 minutes	Medium	Agility
	Stretch	15 minutes	Low	Flexibility
SAT	Aerobic Intervals	1.5 hours	Medium	Anaerobic Threshold
	Strength Workout	1.0 hour	Medium	Strength
	Core Strength	10 minutes	Medium	Trunk Stabilization
	Stretch	15 minutes	Low	Flexibility
SUN	Endurance Workout	2.5 hours	Medium	Endurance
	Balance Workout	30 minutes	Low	Balance
	Stretch	10 minutes	Low	Flexibility

TABLE 10.3 Microcycle 3 | Conditioning Phase

DAY	ACTIVITY	TIME	INTENSITY	INTENT
MON	Visualization	30 minutes	Low	Mental Training
	Stretch	15 minutes	Low	Flexibility
TUES	Soccer	1.0 hour	High	Aerobic/Anaerobic
	Power Workout	45 minutes	High	Power
	Strength Workout	1.0 hour	Medium	Strength
	Core Workout	15 minutes	Medium	Trunk Stabilization
	Stretch	15 minutes	Low	Flexibility
WED	Endurance Workout	2.5 hours	Medium	Endurance
	Stability Workout	30 minutes	Medium	Joint Stabilization
	Stretch	10 minutes	Low	Flexibility
THURS	Tempo Workout	2.0 hours	Medium	Aerobic Capacity
	Core Workout	15 minutes	Medium	Trunk Stabilization
	Stretch	10 minutes	Low	Flexibility
FRI	Easy Aerobic	30 minutes	Low	Recovery
	Agility Workout	30 minutes	Medium	Agility
	Stretch	15 minutes	Low	Flexibility
SAT	Aerobic Intervals	1.5 hours	Medium	Anaerobic Threshold
	Strength Workout	1.0 hour	Medium	Strength
	Core Strength	15 minutes	Medium	Trunk Stabilization
	Stretch	15 minutes	Low	Flexibility
SUN	Endurance Workout	2.5 hours	Medium	Endurance
	Balance Workout	30 minutes	Low	Balance
	Stretch	10 minutes	Low	Flexibility

TABLE 10.4 Microcycle 4 | Conditioning Phase

DAY	ACTIVITY	TIME	INTENSITY	INTENT
MON	Visualization	30 minutes	Low	Mental Training
	Stretch	15 minutes	Low	Flexibility
TUES	Aerobic X-Training	30 minutes	Medium/High	Aerobic/Anaerobic
	Strength Workout	30 minutes	Medium	Strength
	Core Workout	10 minutes	Medium	Trunk Stabilization
	Stretch	15 minutes	Low	Flexibility
WED	Endurance Workout	2.0 hours	Medium	Endurance
	Stability Workout	30 minutes	Medium	Joint Stabilization
	Stretch	10 minutes	Low	Flexibility
THURS	Tempo Workout	1.0 hour	Medium	Aerobic Capacity
	Core Workout	10 minutes	Medium	Trunk Stabilization
	Stretch	10 minutes	Low	Flexibility
FRI	Easy Aerobic	30 minutes	Low	Recovery
	Agility Workout	30 minutes	Medium	Agility
	Stretch	15 minutes	Low	Flexibility
SAT	Aerobic Intervals	1.0 hour	Medium	Anaerobic Threshold
	Strength Workout	30 minutes	Medium	Strength
	Core Strength	10 minutes	Medium	Trunk Stabilization
	Stretch	15 minutes	Low	Flexibility
SUN	Endurance Workout	2.0 hours	Medium	Endurance
	Balance Workout	30 minutes	Low	Balance
	Stretch	10 minutes	Low	Flexibility

BE REALISTIC

Like our goals, our overall training program also needs to be realistic. We need to develop a plan that will help us reach our goals but that we can also live with. If we follow a training program that is too challenging or time-consuming, we run the risk of mental burnout, overtraining, injury, and frustration. Oftentimes, athletes who try to follow a training plan that's too aggressive for them lose a lot of motivation when they are unable to keep up.

Designing a realistic training program may take some experience and trial and error. It's okay to tweak your program slightly if need be until you determine what you can commit to long-term. However, the more thought you put into originally developing your program, the fewer adjustments you'll have to make later.

FOLLOW THROUGH

Following through is obviously extremely important when it comes to attaining any goal. Once we design a realistic and effective training program, we need to make it a priority. If we wake up one morning and decide that we'd rather play golf than go to the gym, our training program will soon lose effectiveness. Any valuable training program will be periodized and will continue to challenge us as our fitness improves. However, if we make a habit of skipping, replacing, shortening, and postponing workouts, we affect the overall volume and intensity of our training.

Since we're only human, there are exceptions to the follow-through rule. If we're feeling ill or very fatigued, it is imperative that we allow ourselves to recover. With experience, we'll be better able to interpret the messages our body sends us and limit the time it takes to regain our form. The general rule is if you don't have the energy to complete a workout with the intensity it deserves, you're better off resting. We need to always be cognizant of cost versus benefit. Chances are the quality of a workout we complete when we're sick or very tired won't warrant delaying the time it takes to feel good again.

We need to be honest with ourselves and be able to distinguish between genuine fatigue and laziness. However, we also need to opt for recovery when appropriate without feeling guilty. Remember, you didn't achieve your level of fitness in one week, and you won't lose it one week, either. If you need to take a few days off, do it and put it behind you. When you start your training program again, don't try to make up the workouts you missed or pick up where you left off. It's best to attempt to get back on track with what you had originally planned to do as quickly as possible so that you follow your intended periodization.

REASSESS

Reassessing our training program is vital. Even if you've been designing training programs for yourself for several years, you'll want to take the time to take an honest look at your training on a regular basis. Are the overload weeks of each macrocycle leaving you ready for a recovery week? Do you feel rested after your recovery weeks? Are you introducing enough variety in your crosstraining to keep your nervous system challenged? Are your workouts becoming monotonous and stale, or are they keeping you engaged?

We need to plan our training effectively, analyze how our body is responding to our training, and reassess the effectiveness of our program from time to time. The end of every microcycle, macrocycle, phase, and season are all good times to reflect on how your training is going. You don't want to continually make changes to your program at the sign of any irregularities. However, at the same time, don't be afraid to make slight adjustments if you're convinced they're warranted, either.

IN THE END

Remember, your results hinge on the effectiveness of your program. Many of us don't take the time necessary to analyze our needs and develop a solid training plan. Think critically, stick with your program, keep things fun, and you'll be well on your way to achieving your goals.

appendix A
training log

monday: / /

RESTING PULSE:

STANDING:

HOURS OF SLEEP:

WEIGHT RATING:

BREAKFAST:

LUNCH:

DINNER:

TRAINING WORKOUTS:

TRAINING FOOD:

HOURS PLANNED:

ACTUAL HOURS:

SUBJECTIVE RATING:

COMMENTS:

tuesday: / /

RESTING PULSE:

BREAKFAST:

TRAINING WORKOUTS:

HOURS PLANNED:

STANDING:

LUNCH:

ACTUAL HOURS:

HOURS OF SLEEP:

TRAINING FOOD:

DINNER:

SUBJECTIVE RATING:

WEIGHT RATING:

COMMENTS:

wednesday: / /

RESTING PULSE:

STANDING:

HOURS OF SLEEP:

WEIGHT RATING:

BREAKFAST:

LUNCH:

DINNER:

TRAINING WORKOUTS:

TRAINING FOOD:

HOURS PLANNED:

ACTUAL HOURS:

SUBJECTIVE RATING:

COMMENTS:

thursday: / /

RESTING PULSE:

BREAKFAST:

TRAINING WORKOUTS:

HOURS PLANNED:

STANDING:

LUNCH:

ACTUAL HOURS:

HOURS OF SLEEP:

TRAINING FOOD:

DINNER:

SUBJECTIVE RATING:

WEIGHT RATING:

COMMENTS:

friday: / /

RESTING PULSE:

BREAKFAST:

TRAINING WORKOUTS:

HOURS PLANNED:

STANDING:

LUNCH:

ACTUAL HOURS:

HOURS OF SLEEP:

TRAINING FOOD:

DINNER:

SUBJECTIVE RATING:

WEIGHT RATING:

COMMENTS:

saturday: / /

RESTING PULSE:

BREAKFAST:

TRAINING WORKOUTS:

HOURS PLANNED:

STANDING:

LUNCH:

ACTUAL HOURS:

HOURS OF SLEEP:

TRAINING FOOD:

DINNER:

SUBJECTIVE RATING:

WEIGHT RATING:

COMMENTS:

sunday: / /

RESTING PULSE:

BREAKFAST:

TRAINING WORKOUTS:

HOURS PLANNED:

STANDING:

LUNCH:

ACTUAL HOURS:

HOURS OF SLEEP:

TRAINING FOOD:

DINNER:

SUBJECTIVE RATING:

WEIGHT RATING:

COMMENTS:

overview | total training hours:

RACE RESULTS/NOTES

COMMENTS ON THE WEEK

GOAL FOR NEXT WEEK

appendix B
35-week training program for a competitive endurance athlete

WEEK		CYCLE	EMPHASIS	PHASE	OBJECTIVE
1	MACRO 1	Micro #1	Low Volume Low Intensity	Conditioning #1	Improve Overall Fitness, Joint Stability, Trunk Stability, and Aerobic Capacity
2		Micro #2	Medium Volume Low Intensity		
3		Micro #3	Medium Volume Medium Intensity		
4		Micro #4	Low Volume Low Intensity		
5	MACRO 2	Micro #1	Medium Volume Low Intensity	Conditioning #2	Improve Overall Fitness, Stability, Strength, and Anaerobic Threshold
6		Micro #2	Medium Volume Medium Intensity		
7		Micro #3	High Volume Medium Intensity		
8		Micro #4	Low Volume Low Intensity		
9	MACRO 3	Micro #1	Medium Volume Low Intensity	Volume Base #1	Improve Endurance, Lactate Threshold, Stability, Strength, and Power
10		Micro #2	Medium Volume Medium Intensity		
11		Micro #3	Medium Volume Medium Intensity		
12		Micro #4	High Volume Medium Intensity		
13		Micro #5	High Volume Medium Intensity		
14		Micro #6	Medium Volume Low Intensity		

NOTE: FOR AN EXAMPLE OF THE CONDITIONING PHASE REFER TO TABLES 10.1 THROUGH 10.4, PAGES 147–50.

WEEK		CYCLE	EMPHASIS	PHASE	OBJECTIVE
15		*Recovery*	*Low Volume* *Low Intensity*	*Recovery*	*Recover*
16	MACRO 4	Micro #1	Medium Volume Low Intensity	Volume Base #2	Improve Endurance, Anaerobic & Lactate Thresholds; Maintain Strength, Stability, Power
17		Micro #2	Medium Volume Medium Intensity		
18		Micro #3	Medium Volume Medium Intensity		
19		Micro #4	High Volume Medium Intensity		
20		Micro #5	High Volume Medium Intensity		
21		Micro #6	High Volume High Intensity		
22		Micro #7	Med Volume Medium Intensity		
23		Micro #8	Low Volume Low Intensity	Volume Base/ Taper	Taper for Peak
24		Peak	Low Volume Medium Intensity	Peak #1	Peak
25		*Recovery #1*	*Low Volume* *Low Intensity*	*Recovery*	*Recover*
26		*Recovery #2*	*Low Volume* *Low Intensity*		

continued

WEEK		CYCLE	EMPHASIS	PHASE	OBJECTIVE
27	MACRO 5	Micro #1	Medium Volume Medium Intensity	Specialization	Improve Speed, Endurance; Maintain Anaerobic & Lactate Thresholds, Strength, Stability, Power
28		Micro #2	High Volume Medium Intensity		
29		Micro #3	High Volume High Intensity		
30		Micro #4	Low Volume Low Intensity		
31	MACRO 6	Micro #1	Medium Volume Low Intensity	Competition	Improve Speed; Maintain Endurance, Anaerobic & Lactate Thresholds, Strength, Stability, Power
32		Micro #2	Medium Volume Medium Intensity		
33		Micro #3	High Volume Medium Intensity		
34		Micro #4	Low Volume Low Intensity	Competition/ Taper	Taper for peak
35		Peak	Low Volume Medium Intensity	Peak #2	Peak

appendix C
32-week training program for a cyclist

WEEK		CYCLE	EMPHASIS	PHASE	OBJECTIVE
1	MACRO 1	Micro #1	Low Volume Low Intensity	Conditioning #1	Fitness, Stability, Aerobic Capacity
2		Micro #2	Medium Volume Low Intensity		
3		Micro #3	Medium Volume Medium Intensity		
4		Micro #4	Low Volume Low Intensity		
5	MACRO 2	Micro #1	Medium Volume Low Intensity	Conditioning #2	Strength Stability, Anaerobic Threshold
6		Micro #2	Medium Volume Medium Intensity		
7		Micro #3	High Volume Medium Intensity		
8		Micro #4	Low Volume Low Intensity		
9	MACRO 3	Micro #1	Medium Volume Low Intensity	Volume Base	Strength, Stability, Endurance
10		Micro #2	Medium Volume Medium Intensity		
11		Micro #3	Medium/High Volume Medium Intensity		
12		Micro #4	High Volume Medium Intensity		
13		Micro #5	Higher Volume Medium Intensity		
14		Micro #6	Highest Volume Medium Intensity		
15		Micro #7	Medium Volume Low Intensity		
16		Micro #8	Low Volume Low Intensity		

WEEK		CYCLE	EMPHASIS	PHASE	OBJECTIVE
17		*Recovery*	*Low Volume* *Low Intensity*	*Recover*	*Recover*
18	MACRO 4	Micro #1	Medium Volume Low Intensity	Specialization	Stability, Power, Lactate Threshold
19		Micro #2	Medium Volume High Intensity		
20	MACRO 5	Micro #1	Medium Volume Low Intensity	Competition	Power, Lactate Threshold, Speed
21		Micro #2	Medium Volume Medium Intensity		
22		Micro #3	High Volume Medium Intensity		
23		Micro #4	Low Volume Low Intensity		
24	MACRO 6	Micro #1	Medium Volume Low Intensity	Competition	Power, Lactate Threshold, Speed
25		Micro #2	Medium Volume Medium Intensity		
26		Micro #3	High Volume Medium Intensity		
27		Micro #4	Low Volume Low Intensity		
28	MACRO 7	Micro #1	Medium Volume Low Intensity	Competition	Power, Lactate Threshold, Speed
29		Micro #2	Medium Volume Medium Intensity		
30		Micro #3	High Volume Medium Intensity		
31		Micro #4	Low Volume Low Intensity	Taper	Taper for Peak
32		Micro #5	Low Volume Medium Intensity	Peak	Peak

Macrocycle 1 | **Microcycle 1** | Conditioning Phase

DAY	ACTIVITY	TIME	INTENSITY	INTENT
MON	Spin or Aerobic Crosstrain	30 min.	Zones 1-2	Aerobic
	Stretch	5 min.	Low	Flexibility
TUES	Aerobic Crosstrain	30 min.	Zones 1-3	Aerobic
	Spin or Aerobic Crosstrain	30 min.	Zones 1-2	Aerobic
	Trunk Stabilization	15 min.	Low	Strength
	Stretch	10 min.	Low	Flexibility
WED	Balance and Agility Workout	45 min.	Zones 1-2	Balance/ Agility
	Joint Stability Workout	45 min.	Medium	Strength/ Stability
	Spin or Aerobic Crosstrain	30 min.	Zones 1-2	Aerobic
	Stretch	15 min.	Low	Flexibility
THURS	Aerobic Crosstrain	30 min.	Zones 1-3	Aerobic
	Spin or Aerobic Crosstrain	30 min.	Zones 1-2	Aerobic
	Trunk Stabilization	15 min.	Low	Strength
	Stretch	10 min.	Low	Flexibility
FRI	Yoga	60 min.	Zones 1-2	Flexibility/ Stability
	Spin or Aerobic Crosstrain	30 min.	Zones 1-2	Aerobic
SAT	Circuit Weights	45 min.	Medium	Strength
	Trunk Stabilization	15 min.	Low	Strength
	Spin or Aerobic Crosstrain	30 min.	Zones 1-2	Aerobic
	Stretch	10 min.	Low	Flexibility
SUN	Spin on Stationary Bike	30 min.	Zones 1-3	Aerobic
	Spin or Aerobic Crosstrain	30 min.	Zones 1-2	Aerobic
	Stretch	10 min.	Low	Flexibility

Macrocycle 1 | **Microcycle 2** | Conditioning Phase

DAY	ACTIVITY	TIME	INTENSITY	INTENT
MON	Spin or Aerobic Crosstrain	30 min.	Zones 1-2	Aerobic
	Stretch	5 min.	Low	Flexibility
TUES	Aerobic Crosstrain	30 min.	Zones 1-3	Aerobic
	Spin or Aerobic Crosstrain	30 min.	Zones 1-2	Aerobic
	Trunk Stabilization	15 min.	Low	Strength
	Stretch	10 min.	Low	Flexibility
WED	Balance and Agility Workout	45 min.	Zones 1-2	Balance/ Agility
	Joint Stability Workout	60 min.	Medium	Strength/ Stability
	Spin or Aerobic Crosstrain	30 min.	Zones 1-2	Aerobic
	Stretch	15 min.	Low	Flexibility
THURS	Aerobic Crosstrain	30 min.	Zones 1-3	Aerobic
	Spin or Aerobic Crosstrain	30 min.	Zones 1-2	Aerobic
	Trunk Stabilization	15 min.	Low	Strength
	Stretch	10 min.	Low	Flexibility
FRI	Yoga	60 min.	Zones 1-2	Flexibility/ Stability
	Spin or Aerobic Crosstrain	30 min.	Zones 1-2	Aerobic
SAT	Circuit Weights	60 min.	Medium	Strength
	Trunk Stabilization	15 min.	Low	Strength
	Spin or Aerobic Crosstrain	30 min.	Zones 1-2	Aerobic
	Stretch	10 min.	Low	Flexibility
SUN	Spin on Stationary Bike	30 min.	Zones 1-3	Aerobic
	Spin or Aerobic Crosstrain	30 min.	Zones 1-2	Aerobic
	Stretch	10 min.	Low	Flexibility

Macrocycle 1 | **Microcycle 3** | Conditioning Phase

DAY	ACTIVITY	TIME	INTENSITY	INTENT
MON	Spin or Aerobic Crosstrain	30 min.	Zones 1-2	Aerobic
	Stretch	5 min.	Low	Flexibility
TUES	Aerobic Crosstrain	30 min.	Zones 1-3	Aerobic
	Spin or Aerobic Crosstrain	30 min.	Zones 1-2	Aerobic
	Trunk Stabilization	15 min.	Low	Strength
	Stretch	10 min.	Low	Flexibility
WED	Balance and Agility Workout	45 min.	Zones 1-2	Balance/ Agility
	Strength and Stability Workout	75 min.	Medium	Strength/ Stability
	Spin or Aerobic Crosstrain	30 min.	Zones 1-2	Aerobic
	Stretch	15 min.	Low	Flexibility
THURS	Aerobic Crosstrain	30 min.	Zones 1-3	Aerobic
	Spin or Aerobic Crosstrain	30 min.	Zones 1-2	Aerobic
	Trunk Stabilization	15 min.	Low	Strength
	Stretch	10 min.	Low	Flexibility
FRI	Yoga	60 min.	Zones 1-2	Flexibility/ Stability
	Spin or Aerobic Crosstrain	30 min.	Zones 1-2	Aerobic
SAT	Strength and Stability Workout	75 min.	Medium	Strength/ Stability
	Trunk Stabilization	15 min.	Low	Strength
	Spin or Aerobic Crosstrain	30 min.	Zones 1-2	Aerobic
	Stretch	10 min.	Low	Flexibility
SUN	Spin on Stationary Bike	30 min.	Zones 1-3	Aerobic
	Spin or Aerobic Crosstrain	30 min.	Zones 1-2	Aerobic
	Stretch	10 min.	Low	Flexibility

Macrocycle 1 | **Microcycle 4** | Conditioning Phase

DAY	ACTIVITY	TIME	INTENSITY	INTENT
MON	**OFF**			
TUES	Aerobic Crosstrain	30 min.	Zones 1-3	Aerobic
	Spin or Aerobic Crosstrain	30 min.	Zones 1-2	Aerobic
	Trunk Stabilization	15 min.	Low	Strength
	Stretch	10 min.	Low	Flexibility
WED	Balance and Agility Workout	45 min.	Zones 1-2	Balance/ Agility
	Joint Stability Workout	45 min.	Medium	Strength/ Stability
	Spin or Aerobic Crosstrain	30 min.	Zones 1-2	Aerobic
	Stretch	15 min.	Low	Flexibility
THURS	Aerobic Crosstrain	30 min.	Zones 1-3	Aerobic
	Spin or Aerobic Crosstrain	30 min.	Zones 1-2	Aerobic
	Trunk Stabilization	15 min.	Low	Strength
	Stretch	10 min.	Low	Flexibility
FRI	Yoga	60 min.	Zones 1-2	Flexibility/ Stability
SAT	Circuit Weights	45 min.	Medium	Strength
	Trunk Stabilization	15 min.	Low	Strength
	Spin or Aerobic Crosstrain	30 min.	Zones 1-2	Aerobic
	Stretch	15 min.	Low	Flexibility
SUN	Spin on Stationary Bike	30 min.	Zones 1-3	Aerobic
	Spin or Aerobic Crosstrain	30 min.	Zones 1-2	Aerobic
	Stretch	10 min.	Low	Flexibility

appendix D
26-week training overview for a nordic skier

WEEK		CYCLE	EMPHASIS	PHASE	OBJECTIVE
1	MACRO 1	Micro #1	Low Volume Low Intensity	Conditioning #1	Fitness, Stability, Aerobic Capacity
2		Micro #2	Medium Volume Low Intensity		
3		Micro #3	Medium Volume Medium Intensity		
4		Micro #4	Low Volume Low Intensity		
5	MACRO 2	Micro #1	Medium Volume Low Intensity	Conditioning #2	Strength, Stability, Anaerobic Threshold
6		Micro #2	Medium Volume Medium Intensity		
7		Micro #3	High Volume Medium Intensity		
8		Micro #4	Low Volume Low Intensity		
9	MACRO 3	Micro #1	Medium Volume Low Intensity	Volume Base	Strength, Endurance, Stability
10		Micro #2	Medium Volume Medium Intensity		
11		Micro #3	Medium Volume Medium Intensity		
12		Micro #4	High Volume Medium Intensity		
13		Micro #5	High Volume Medium Intensity		
14		Micro #6	Medium Volume Low Intensity		

WEEK		CYCLE	EMPHASIS	PHASE	OBJECTIVE
15		*Recovery*	*Low Volume* *Low Intensity*	*Recovery*	*Recover*
16	MACRO 4	Micro #1	Medium Volume Medium Intensity	Specialization	Strength, Power, Lactate Threshold
17		Micro #2	Medium Volume High Intensity		
18	MACRO 5	Micro #1	Medium Volume Low Intensity	Competition #1	Power, Lactate Threshold, Speed
19		Micro #2	Medium Volume Medium Intensity		
20		Micro #3	High Volume Medium Intensity		
21		Micro #4	Low Volume Low Intensity		
22	MACRO 6	Micro #1	Medium Volume Low Intensity	Competition #2	Power, Lactate Threshold, Speed
23		Micro #2	Medium Volume Medium Intensity		
24		Micro #3	High Volume Medium Intensity		
25		Micro #4	Low Volume Low Intensity	Taper	Taper for Peak
26		Micro #5	Low Volume Medium Intensity	Peak	Peak

Macrocycle 3 | **Microcycle 1** | Base Miles Phase

DAY	ACTIVITY	TIME	INTENSITY	INTENT
MON	**Off**			
TUES	Anaerobic Intervals	45 min.	Zones 1-4	Improve LT
	Strength/Stability Workout	45 min.	Medium	Strength
	Stretch	15 min.	Low	Flexibility
WED	Endurance	1.5 hr.	Zones 1-3	Endurance
	Stretch	15 min.	Low	Flexibility
THURS	Tempo	60 min.	Zones 1-3	Aerobic
	Stretch	15 min.	Low	Flexibility
FRI	Active Rest	30 min.	Zone 1	Active Rest
	Stretch	15 min.	Low	Flexibility
SAT	Aerobic Intervals	45 min.	Zones 1-3	Improve AT
	Strength/Stability Workout	45 min.	Medium	Strength
	Stretch	15 min.	Low	Flexibility
SUN	Endurance and Hill Work	1.5 hr.	Zones 1-3	Endurance
	Stretch	15 min.	Low	Flexibility

Macrocycle 3 | **Microcycle 2** | Base Miles Phase

DAY	ACTIVITY	TIME	INTENSITY	INTENT
MON	**Off**			
TUES	Anaerobic Intervals	60 min.	Zones 1-4	Improve LT
	Strength/Stability Workout	45 min.	Medium	Strength
	Stretch	15 min.	Low	Flexibility
WED	Endurance	1.75 hr.	Zones 1-3	Endurance
	Stretch	15 min.	Low	Flexibility
THURS	Tempo	60 min.	Zones 1-3	Aerobic
	Trunk Workout	15 min.	Low	Trunk Strength
	Stretch	15 min.	Low	Flexibility
FRI	Active Rest	30 min.	HR Zone 1	Active Rest
	Stretch	15 min.	Low	Flexibility
SAT	Aerobic Intervals	60 min.	Zones 1-3	Improve AT
	Strength/Stability Workout	45 min.	Medium	Strength
	Stretch	15 min.	Low	Flexibility
SUN	Endurance and Hill Work	1.5 hr.	Zones 1-3	Endurance
	Stretch	15 min.	Low	Flexibility

Macrocycle 3 | **Microcycle 3** | Base Miles Phase

DAY	ACTIVITY	TIME	INTENSITY	INTENT
MON	Active Rest	30 min.	Zone 1	Active Rest
	Stretch	15 min.	Low	Flexibility
TUES	Anaerobic Intervals	60 min.	Zones 1-4	Improve LT
	Strength/Stability	45 min.	Medium	Strength
	Stretch	15 min.	Low	Flexibility
WED	Endurance	1.75 hr.	Zones 1-3	Endurance
	Stretch	15 min.	Low	Flexibility
THURS	Tempo	75 min.	Zones 1-3	Aerobic
	Trunk Workout	15 min.	Low	Trunk Strength
	Stretch	15 min.	Low	Flexibility
FRI	Active Rest	30 min.	Zone 1	Active Rest
	Stretch	15 min.	Low	Flexibility
SAT	Aerobic Intervals	60 min.	Zones 1-3	Improve AT
	Strength/Stability	45 min.	Medium	Strength
	Stretch	15 min.	Low	Flexibility
SUN	Endurance and Hill Work	1.75 hr.	Zones 1-3	Endurance
	Stretch	15 min.	Low	Flexibility

Macrocycle 3 | **Microcycle 4** | Base Miles Phase

DAY	ACTIVITY	TIME	INTENSITY	INTENT
MON	Active Rest	30 min.	Zone 1	Active Rest
	Stretch	15 min.	Low	Flexibility
TUES	Anaerobic Intervals	60 min.	Zones 1-4	Improve LT
	Strength/Stability Workout	45 min.	Medium	Strength
	Stretch	15 min.	Low	Flexibility
WED	Endurance	2.0 hr.	Zones 1-3	Endurance
	Stretch	15 min.	Low	Flexibility
THURS	Tempo	1.5 hr.	Zones 1-3	Aerobic
	Trunk Workout	15 min.	Low	Trunk Strength
	Stretch	15 min.	Low	Flexibility
FRI	Active Rest	45 min.	Zone 1	Active Rest
	Stretch	15 min.	Low	Flexibility
SAT	Aerobic Intervals	60 min.	Zones 1-3	Improve AT
	Strength/Stability Workout	45 min.	Medium	Strength
	Stretch	15 min.	Low	Flexibility
SUN	Endurance and Hill Work	2.0 hr.	Zones 1-3	Endurance
	Stretch	15 min.	Low	Flexibility

Macrocycle 3 | **Microcycle 5** | Base Miles Phase

DAY	ACTIVITY	TIME	INTENSITY	INTENT
MON	Active Rest	30 min.	Zone 1	Active Rest
	Stretch	15 min.	Low	Flexibility
TUES	Anaerobic Intervals	60 min.	Zones 1-4	Improve LT
	Strength/Stability Workout	45 min.	Medium	Strength
	Stretch	15 min.	Low	Flexibility
WED	Endurance	2.5 hr.	Zones 1-3	Endurance
	Stretch	15 min.	Low	Flexibility
THURS	Tempo	1.5 hr.	Zones 1-3	Aerobic
	Trunk Workout	15 min.	Low	Trunk Strength
	Stretch	15 min.	Low	Flexibility
FRI	Active Rest	45 min.	Zone 1	Active Rest
	Stretch	15 min.	Low	Flexibility
SAT	Aerobic Intervals	60 min.	Zones 1-3	Improve AT
	Strength/Stability Workout	45 min.	Medium	Strength
	Stretch	15 min.	Low	Flexibility
SUN	Endurance and Hill Work	2.5 hr.	Zones 1-3	Endurance
	Stretch	15 min.	Low	Flexibility

Macrocycle 3 | **Microcycle 6** | Base Miles Phase

DAY	ACTIVITY	TIME	INTENSITY	INTENT
MON	**Off**			
TUES	Anaerobic Intervals	45 min.	Zones 1-4	Improve LT
	Strength/Stability Workout	45 min.	Medium	Strength
	Stretch	15 min.	Low	Flexibility
WED	Endurance	1.5 hr.	Zones 1-3	Endurance
	Stretch	15 min.	Low	Flexibility
THURS	Tempo	60 min.	Zones 1-3	Aerobic
	Stretch	15 min.	Low	Flexibility
FRI	Active Rest	30 min.	Zone 1	Active Rest
	Stretch	15 min.	Low	Flexibility
SAT	Aerobic Intervals	45 min.	Zones 1-3	Improve AT
	Strength/Stability Workout	45 min.	Medium	Strength
	Stretch	15 min.	Low	Flexibility
SUN	Endurance and Hill Work	1.5 hr.	Zones 1-3	Endurance
	Stretch	15 min.	Low	Flexibility

appendix E
crosstraining workouts

BALANCE WORKOUT EXAMPLES

Workout #1: 15-minute workout

(15 SETS WITH 15-SECOND REST BETWEEN EACH SET)

EXERCISE	SET X REP
Balls of feet on edge of step with eyes closed	3 x 45 sec.
Reach down and rotate back while standing on one leg on a half foam roll	4 x 45 sec.
Partner tug-of-war standing on one leg on half foam rolls	4 x 45 sec.
Walking on a narrow beam, railing, or tightrope	2 x 45 sec.
Unstable surface obstacle course	2 x 45 sec.

Workout #2: 15-minute workout

(15 SETS WITH 15-SECOND REST BETWEEN EACH SET)

EXERCISE	SET X REP
Heels of feet on edge of step with eyes closed	3 x 45 sec.
Reach down/rotate back standing on one leg on a half foam roll: hold medicine ball	4 x 45 sec.
Partner tug-of-war standing on one leg on full foam rolls	4 x 45 sec.
Logroll a full foam roll forward	2 x 45 sec.
Half squats on a balance board while throwing a medicine ball to partner	2 x 45 sec.

Workout #3: 15-minute workout

(15 SETS WITH 15-SECOND REST BETWEEN EACH SET)

EXERCISE	SET X REP
Reach and rotate while standing on one leg on a disc	4 x 45 sec.
Logroll a full foam roll backward	2 x 45 sec.
Full squats on a balance board while throwing a medicine ball to partner	3 x 45 sec.
Half squats on a stability ball while throwing a medicine ball to partner	3 x 45 sec.
Walking on a narrow beam, railing, or tightrope while holding a medicine ball	3 x 45 sec.

Workout #4: 15-minute workout

(15 SETS WITH 15-SECOND REST BETWEEN EACH SET)

EXERCISE	SET X REP
Reach/rotate standing on one leg on an unstable surface: hold medicine ball	4 x 45 sec.
Half squats on balance board while throwing a medicine ball to partner with one arm	2 x 45 sec.
Full squats on a stability ball while throwing a medicine ball to partner	3 x 45 sec.
Walking on a narrow beam, railing, or tightrope: throw a medicine ball to partner	3 x 45 sec.
Logroll a full foam roll forward and backward	3 x 45 sec.

Workout #5: 15-minute workout

(15 SETS WITH 15-SECOND REST BETWEEN EACH SET)

EXERCISE	SET X REP
Logroll a full foam roll forward and backward while holding a medicine ball	3 x 45 sec.
Full squats on balance board while throwing a medicine ball to partner with one arm	3 x 45 sec.
Half squats on stability ball while throwing a medicine ball to partner with one arm	3 x 45 sec.
Logroll a full foam roll forward while throwing a medicine ball to partner	3 x 45 sec.
Unstable surface obstacle course while holding a medicine ball	3 x 45 sec.

JOINT STABILIZATION WORKOUT EXAMPLES

Workout #1: 15-minute workout

(15 SETS WITH 30-SECOND REST BETWEEN EACH SET)

EXERCISE	SET X REP
Single-leg bench dip	4 x 15 (2X PER LEG)
Push-ups on two Dyna discs: one foot in air, one on ground	2 x 30 (15X PER LEG)
Forward lunge with back foot on ball	4 x 15 (2X PER LEG)
Standing push-ups on stability ball: neutral spine, one foot on ground, one in air	2 x 30 (15X PER LEG)
Half squats on Bosu Ball: watch knee tracking	3 x 15

Workout #2: 15-minute workout

(15 SETS WITH 30-SECOND REST BETWEEN EACH SET)

EXERCISE	SET X REP
Stability ball push-ups: hands on bench, one foot on stability ball	3 x 20 (10X PER LEG)
Half squats on a lateral balance board	3 x 20
Cable shoulder internal rotation	3 x 20
Quarter squats while standing on stability ball	3 x 30 sec.
Cable shoulder external rotation	3 x 20

Workout #3: 15-minute workout

(15 SETS WITH 30-SECOND REST BETWEEN EACH SET)

EXERCISE	SET X REP
Single-leg quarter squats on Bosu Ball: level hips	4 x 15 (2X PER LEG)
Dumbbell shoulder lateral raise	3 x 20
Full squats on a lateral balance board	3 x 30 sec.
Dumbbell shoulder forward raise	3 x 20
Half squats on full foam roll	2 x 20

Workout #4: 15-minute workout

(15 SETS WITH 30-SECOND REST BETWEEN EACH SET)

EXERCISE	SET X REP
Single-leg half squats on Bosu Ball: level hips	4 x 15 (2X PER LEG)
Stability ball push-ups: hands on ball, one foot on bench	3 x 20 (10X PER LEG)
Half squats while standing on stability ball	2 x 30 sec.
Dumbbell shoulder punches: extend dumbbells in all directions	2 x 30 sec.
Lateral lunges onto an unstable surface (such as a Dyna disc)	4 x 20 (2X PER LEG)

Workout #5: 15-minute workout

(15 SETS WITH 30-SECOND REST BETWEEN EACH SET)

EXERCISE	SET X REP
Dynamic hip and glute pull: stand on opposite leg	4 x 15 (2X PER LEG)
Push-ups on lateral balance board: hands on board, one foot on ground, one in air	2 x 20 (10X PER LEG)
Full squats while standing on stability ball	3 x 15
Single-arm dumbbell bench press while bridging on ball	4 x 15 (2X PER ARM)
Full squats on full foam roll	2 x 20

TRUNK STRENGTH/STABILIZATION WORKOUT EXAMPLES

Workout #1: 10-minute workout

(7 ONE-MINUTE SETS WITH 30-SECOND REST BETWEEN EACH SET)

EXERCISE	SET X REP
Single-leg lowering: off end of bench; keep pelvis stable	1 x 60 sec.
Cable pull obliques: keep knees bent and arms straight	2 x 60 sec. (1 MIN. EACH SIDE)
Stability ball preacher rollouts: roll ball out with arms while kneeling	1 x 60 sec.
Back extensions: maintain a neutral spine for the entire range of motion	1 x 60 sec.
Dynamic quadruped: while on all fours, extend arm and opposite leg out	2 x 60 sec

Workout #2: 15-minute workout

(10 ONE-MINUTE SETS WITH 30-SECOND REST BETWEEN EACH SET)

EXERCISE	SET X REP
Leg circles: with small stability ball between feet; 30 seconds each direction	2 x 60 sec.
Side stability ball crunches: feet against wall, hips on ball, crunch up slowly	2 x 60 sec.
Pikes on bench: while lying on back, kick legs up straight toward ceiling	2 x 60 sec.
Back extensions while holding a medicine ball: maintain a neutral spine	2 x 60 sec.
#1 kneel on stability ball; #2 kneel on stability ball with eyes closed, use spotter	2 x 60 sec.

Workout #3: 15-minute workout

(10 ONE-MINUTE SETS WITH 30-SECOND REST BETWEEN EACH SET)

EXERCISE	SET X REP
#1 single-leg lowering; #2 single/double-leg lowering; #3 double leg only	3 x 60 sec.
Side crunches: one foot on stability ball, crunch up and roll ball in at same time	2 x 60 (1X EACH SIDE)
Crunches over ball: hold medicine ball over head, up and down slow	3 x 60 sec.
Prone cobra on ball with dumbbells: #1 bring dumbbells out to side; #2 raise dumbbells out front	2 x 60 sec.

Workout #4: 15-minute workout

(10 ONE-MINUTE SETS WITH 30-SECOND REST BETWEEN EACH SET)

EXERCISE	SET X REP
Hanging abs: #1 crunch knees bent; #2 side crunches; #3 leg circles (30 seconds each direction)	3 x 60 sec.
Stability ball leg rollouts: #1 alternate rolling side to side; #2 roll straight in	2 x 60 sec.
#1 swimmers; #2 dynamic quadruped on ball; #3 dynamic quadruped on foam roll	3 x 60 sec.
Bridge on ball: alternate one leg kick, kick out, to the side, back in, then down	2 x 60 sec.

Workout #5: 15-minute workout

(10 ONE-MINUTE SETS WITH 30-SECOND REST BETWEEN EACH SET)

EXERCISE	SET X REP
#1 leg circles (30 seconds each direction); #2 single-leg lowering on incline bench	2 x 60 sec.
#1 full crunches: on bench; #2 side crunches on ball: hold 10-pound weights	2 x 60 sec. (30 EACH SIDE)
#1 V-ups; #2 V-ups while holding a medicine ball	2 x 60 sec.
Stability ball shoulder rolls: bridge on ball, roll slowly from side to side	1 x 60 sec.

AGILITY WORKOUT EXAMPLES

Workout #1: 30-minute lower-body workout

(25 SETS WITH 30-60-SECOND REST BETWEEN SETS)

EXERCISE	SET X REP
Ankle bounces: on soft surface, with slight bend in the knees, fast tempo	4 x 30
Double leg stair hops: skip 1 or 2 stairs, land soft and controlled	5 x 10
Jump rope side to side while moving down a line, forward and backward	5 x 30
Single leg forward stair hops: skip 1 or 2 stairs, land soft, watch knee tracking	6 x 10 (3X EACH LEG)
Split squat jumps: jump from a lunge position, land with opposite leg forward	5 x 20 (10 EACH SIDE)

Workout #2: 30-minute upper body workout

(25 SETS WITH 30-60-SECOND REST BETWEEN SETS)

EXERCISE	SET X REP
Explosive overhead medicine ball throw to partner or against a trampoline: standing	5 x 15
Clapping push-ups: on soft surface, maintain neutral spine, fast tempo	5 x 15
Explosive tricep medicine ball throws to a partner or against a trampoline while kneeling	5 x 15
Explosive 45-degree pull-up: maintain neutral spine	5 x 10
Explosive medicine ball bench push-ups with a partner: maintain neutral spine	5 x 10

Workout #3: 30-minute lower-body workout

(25 SETS WITH 30-60-SECOND REST BETWEEN SETS)

EXERCISE	SET X REP
Broad jumps: land soft and controlled, watch knee tracking	5 x 10
Tuck jumps: bring knees up to chest, fast tempo	4 x 15
Single-leg broad jumps: land soft and controlled, watch knee tracking	6 x 10 (3X EACH LEG)
Single-leg lateral stair hops: skip 1 or 2 stairs, land soft, watch knee tracking	6 x 10 (3X EACH LEG)
Vertical jumps: jump as high as you can, land soft and controlled	4 x 10

Workout #4: 30-minute upper-body workout

(25 SETS WITH 30–60-SECOND REST BETWEEN SETS)

EXERCISE	SET X REP
Single-arm medicine ball throws to a partner or against a trampoline: standing	6 x 15 (3X EACH ARM)
Explosive overhead medicine ball throw to a partner or against a trampoline: stand on one leg	5 x 20 (10 X EACH LEG)
Explosive fixed bar incline press: have spotter keep bar from twisting, fast tempo	4 x 15 (5 SLOW, 10 EXPLOSIVE)
Explosive rows on rowing machine: pull fast, return slow, maintain neutral spine	5 x 10
Explosive medicine ball chest press with a partner: laying down, partner stands above	5 x 15

Workout #5: 30-minute upper/lower-body workout

(25 SETS WITH 30-60-SECOND REST BETWEEN SETS)

EXERCISE	SET X REP
Jump rope four-square: jump side to side, lateral and diagonal	5 x 30
Single-arm medicine ball throws to partner or against a trampoline: stand on one leg	6 x 20 (3 EACH ARM, 10 EACH LEG)
Lateral jumps over a bench: land soft, minimize time on the ground	4 x 10
Explosive medicine ball push-ups: one hand on ball, roll ball to other side as you push-up	5 x 10 (5 EACH SIDE)
Split squat jumps while holding a medicine ball: maintain neutral spine, watch knee tracking	5 x 20 (10 EACH SIDE)

STRENGTH WORKOUT EXAMPLES

Workout #1: 30-minute lower-body workout

(25 SETS WITH 30-60-SECOND REST BETWEEN SETS)

EXERCISE	SET X REP
Dumbbell matrix lunges: alternate lunging forward, to the side and rear diagonally	3 x 18 (3 X 6 LUNGES)
Single-leg wall sit dips: down to 90 degrees; place stability ball behind back against wall	6 x 12 (3X EACH LEG)
Eccentric hamstrings: lower for a count of 5, maintain a neutral spine	1 x 5 / 1 x 6 1 x 8 / 1 x 5
Single-leg calf raises: stand on edge of step, use full range of motion	6 x 20 (3X EACH LEG)
Hip fexor cable pull: strap around ankle, step and drive knee, use arms	6 x 10 (3X EACH LEG)

Workout #2: 30-minute upper-body workout

(25 SETS WITH 30-60-SECOND REST BETWEEN SETS)

EXERCISE	SET X REP
Seated rows: neutral spine, relax traps, squeeze shoulder blades, slow tempo	1 x 10 / 1 x 8 2 x 6 / 1 x 10
Assisted pull-up machine: alternate grip at the top of every rep, relax traps	5 x 15
Double-leg stability ball hamstrings: heels on ball, raise/lower hips slowly	5 x 15
Dumbbell press while bridging on stability ball: keep hips up, slow tempo	1 x 10 / 1 x 8 2 x 6 / 1 x 10
Standing row: from half squat, keep neutral spine, squeeze shoulder blades	1 x 10 / 1 x 8 2 x 6 / 1 x 10

Workout #3: 30-minute lower-body workout

(25 SETS WITH 30-60-SECOND REST BETWEEN SETS)

EXERCISE	SET X REP
Single-leg stability ball hamstrings: place one heel on ball, raise/lower hips slowly	4 x 15 (3X EACH LEG)
Single-leg leg press with a Dyna disc: use full range of motion, watch knee tracking	6 x 10 (3X EACH LEG)
Single-leg cable leg curl: maintain neutral spine, watch knee tracking, slow tempo	6 x 10 (3X EACH LEG)
Single-leg fixed bar squat: maintain neutral spine and level hips, watch knee tracking, slow tempo	6 x 10 (3X EACH LEG)
Partner resisted tibialis anterior: have partner resist in both directions	3 x 20

Workout #4: 30-minute upper-body workout

(25 SETS WITH 30–60-SECOND REST BETWEEN SETS)

EXERCISE	SET X REP
Front lat pulldown: relax traps, neutral spine, squeeze shoulder blades	1 x 10 / 1 x 8 2 x 6 / 1 x 10
Dumbbell arm curls while kneeling on stability ball: alternate arms, slow tempo	3 x 20 (10X EACH ARM)
Bench press: with feet up and legs bent at 90 degrees, slow tempo	1 x 10 / 1 x 8 2 x 6 / 1 x 10
Single-arm standing cable butterfly: maintain neutral spine, relax traps, slow tempo	6 x 10 (3X EACH ARM)
Single-arm standing cable press: maintain neutral spine, relax traps, slow tempo	6 x 10 (3X EACH ARM)

Workout #5: 30-minute upper/lower-body workout

(25 SETS WITH 30-60-SECOND REST BETWEEN SETS)

EXERCISE	SET X REP
Single-leg seated leg curls: maintain neutral spine, watch knee tracking, slow tempo	6 x 10 (3X EACH LEG)
Incline dumbbell bench press: maintain neutral spine, slow tempo	1 x 10 / 1 x 8 1 x 6 / 1 x 10
Leg press: lower for a count of 5, watch knee tracking, slow tempo	6 x 10 (3X EACH LEG)
Single-arm/single-leg standing cable pull: stand on opposite leg, relax traps, slow tempo	6 x 10 (3X EACH ARM)
Back squat: maintain neutral spine, watch knee tracking, slow tempo	1 x 10 / 1 x 8 1 x 10

POWER WORKOUT EXAMPLES

Workout #1: 30-minute lower-body workout

(25 SETS WITH 30-60-SECOND REST BETWEEN SETS)

EXERCISE	SET X REP
Ankle bounces: on soft surface, with slight bend in the knees, fast tempo	4 x 30
Double leg stair hops: skip 1 or 2 stairs, land soft and controlled	5 x 10
Jump rope side to side while moving down a line: forward and backward	5 x 30
Single-leg forward stair hops: skip 1 or 2 stairs, land soft, watch knee tracking	6 x 10 (3X EACH LEG)
Split squat jumps: jump from a lunge position, land with opposite leg forward	5 x 20 (10 EACH SIDE)

Workout #2: 30-minute upper-body workout

(25 SETS WITH 30-60-SECOND REST BETWEEN SETS)

EXERCISE	SET X REP
Explosive overhead medicine ball throw to partner or against trampoline: standing	5 x 15
Clapping push-ups: on soft surface, maintain neutral spine, fast tempo	5 x 15
Explosive tricep medicine ball throws to partner or against trampoline: kneeling	5 x 15
Explosive 45-degree pull-up: maintain neutral spine	5 x 10
Explosive medicine ball bench push-ups with a partner: maintain neutral spine	5 x 10

Workout #3: 30-minute lower-body workout

(25 SETS WITH 30-60-SECOND REST BETWEEN SETS)

EXERCISE	SET X REP
Broad jumps: land soft and controlled, watch knee tracking	5 x 10
Tuck jumps: bring knees up into chest, fast tempo	4 x 15
Single-leg broad jumps: land soft and controlled, watch knee tracking	6 x 10 (3X EACH LEG)
Single-leg lateral stair hops: skip 1 or 2 stairs, land soft, watch knee tracking	6 x 10 (3X EACH LEG)
Vertical jumps: jump as high as you can, land soft and controlled	4 x 10

Workout #4: 30-minute upper-body workout

(25 SETS WITH 30-60-SECOND REST BETWEEN SETS)

EXERCISE	SET X REP
Single-arm medicine ball throws to a partner or against a trampoline: standing	6 x 15 (3X EACH ARM)
Explosive overhead medicine ball throw to a partner or against a trampoline: stand on one leg	5 x 20 (10 EACH LEG)
Explosive fixed bar incline press: have spotter keep bar from twisting, fast tempo	4 x 15 (5 SLOW, 10 EXPLOSIVE)
Explosive rows on rowing machine: pull fast, return slow, maintain neutral spine	5 x 10
Medicine ball explosive partner chest press: laying down, partner stands above	5 x 15

index

about the author

Raul Guisado's unique and proven approach to strength and conditioning has been developed through a combination of his athletic experience, education, and success as an Olympic coach. He grew up in California to become an accomplished bicycle racer, ski racer, and surfer and has been coaching athletes in a variety of sports since 1989. Raul studied kinesiology at Colorado University–Boulder, has a degree in physiology from the University of California–Santa Barbara, and is pursuing a graduate degree in sport psychology. He is a U.S. Cycling Federation–licensed expert cycling coach, a U.S. Skiing Association professional ski coach, and a certified strength and conditioning specialist. From 1995 to 1999, Raul worked for the U.S. Ski Team as a World Cup/Olympic coach and strength and conditioning coach. He was a coach in the 1998 and 2002 Winter Olympic Games and will be coaching at the 2006 Winter Olympic Games.